"A hilarious lampoon of Hollywood, the Valley and the whole L.A. scene: the industry, the people, the self-absorption."

—*USA Today*

"If Oscar Wilde could be brought back to life and persuaded to visit Los Angeles with Hunter Thompson as his guide, one wonders if even he could do satiric justice to the place (justice being a malleable concept, as any Angeleno can tell you) the way Sandra Tsing Loh has in this collection of essays. Hers is monster talent; this book represents the appearance of a seemingly inexhaustible source of tooth-gnashing discouragement to the rest of us, who must try (and usually fail) to be witty. Even her acknowledgments left me begging for mercy; don't read this book in a place where you are expected to keep quiet."

—Mark Salzman, author of *Iron* and *Silk*

"A wonderfully funny writer. You will like her so much that you will be tempted to put her book inside your body. Don't. Remain decorous. Simply bask in the honeyed light of the Sandra afterglow."　　　　—Henry Alford, author of *Municipal Bondage*

"In these days, when the short humorous essay has devolved to a plodding reminiscence leading up to a rickety punch line, a passel of puns, or a romp through the thesaurus, Tsing Loh's pieces have an electric crackle and a stink of L.A. smog that put *The New Yorker* back page in its place."

—Daniel Pinkwater, author of *The Afterlife Diet*

Continued . . .

"Tsing Loh [is] a wisecracking literary cousin to Merrill Markoe and Carrie Fisher . . . a sharp, earthy observer of an eccentric world." —*Kirkus Reviews*

"She's funny, urban and self-deprecating. She's a wicked cultural observer given to sarcastic one-liners. She's jaded—and proud of it. Dorothy Parker? Fran Lebowitz? Nora Ephron? Well, no. Her name is Sandra Tsing Loh. You may not know the name yet, but chances are that you will. She's that good." —*Buffalo News*

"For all their frothy charm, her musings on the plight of an over-educated, underemployed generation that measures success in terms of the ability to afford health insurance are often as insightful as they are witty. . . . [A] sardonic but never mean-spirited take on modern urban life." —*Publishers Weekly*

"Cool, quick, trend-conscious and ironic . . . [she has] an unerring eye for where to stick the needle that punctures social pretentions." —*Toronto Globe and Mail*

"Just when you thought life wasn't all that funny anymore, along comes Sandra Tsing Loh. She's here to cheer us up."
—*The Arizona Daily Star*

"Insightful and hilarious . . . She's a natural commentator with an acute eye and a talent for humor. *Depth Takes a Holiday* would be a great book to take to the beach." —*The Toronto Star*

"Funny, wonderfully mean and suspiciously wise."
—*San Diego Union-Tribune*

Depth
Takes a
Holiday

Essays from
Lesser
Los Angeles

Sandra Tsing Loh

RIVERHEAD BOOKS

NEW YORK

RIVERHEAD BOOKS
Published by The Berkley Publishing Group
200 Madison Avenue
New York, NY 10016

Riverhead hardcover edition: April 1996
First Riverhead trade paperback edition: August 1997
Riverhead trade paperback edition ISBN: 1-57322-611-4

The Putnam Berkley World Wide Web site address is http://www.berkley.com

The Library of Congress has catalogued the Riverhead hardcover edition as follows:

Loh, Sandra Tsing.
Depth takes a holiday: essays from lesser Los Angeles /
Sandra Tsing Loh.
p.   cm.
ISBN 1-57322-031-0 (acid-free paper)
1. Los Angeles (Calif.)—Humor.   I. Title.
PN6231.C16L64   1996   95-44922 CIP
814'.54—dc20

Printed in the United States of America

10 9 8 7 6 5 4 3 2 1

Acknowledgments

My thanks to my first writing teacher, T. Coraghessan Boyle. Look how shamelessly I continue to drop his name after all these years.

My thanks to Jonathan Gold for giving me my first writing assignment at the *L.A. Weekly* in 1985. Sorry about the lawsuit.

My thanks to my agent, Sloan "Whatever Happened to Trying?" Harris at ICM. Sloan kindly took me on when I was nothing—nothing! A mere ant whose line printer could not type the letter *i*. But hey, if he's my agent, maybe he could be yours, too! Call him today at 1-900-556-5600! (Perhaps not, but I've always thought such a notion would look quite startling in print.)

My thanks to my loyal writer friends. Not the disloyal ones: to you I thumb my nose. (Also, contrary to your nasty critiques of my work, I do not use *too many* italics—I feel I use *too few*.) Standing the test of stress are Mel Green, Beverly Olevin, and (Hollywood Insider) Donald Rawley. Standing the test of time is my best friend, Teresa Yunker. Special thanks, too, to Dan Akst, who came up with this book's title in ten seconds, while I spent a month and came up with nothing. I hate you, Dan.

My biggest thanks of all, however, must go to *Buzz* magazine, where most of these essays first appeared. *Buzz* kindly took me on when I was nothing—nothing! A mere ant whose . . . To brilliant and lovable Greg Critser I owe everything; to pectoraliginous Non-Neapolitan (a.k.a.: Fabio's Dark Other) Allan Mayer I may owe even more. But the most pathetic, cringing gratitude must go to Renee "The Velvet Hammer" Vogel. Without Renee's tireless Love Faxes, I quite simply would not want to go on.

The wave of my huge *Buzz* gratitude then crests and crashes before the radiant Glinda-the-Good bubble that contains my Riverhead editor, Mary South.

And of course, final thanks to my wonderful family, whose lives, as always, have been pillaged for this book. You know who you are.

Contents

Part Three

LIFE IN THE CITY

My World: A Defense

Recently I received a letter in response to my *Buzz* magazine column which caused me to slump forward in defeat. To wit:

> It's such a comfort to know that a witty mind like yours is at work in the *deadlands of Southern California*. That there are active brain cells busy working away somewhere in this *hinterland of the proudly uninformed* (italics mine).

There was more:

> I frequently feel so trapped in L.A. and crave all that brilliance and immediacy I knew back in NYC. I assume you've probably lived back east, or else there's no way you could have developed such an informed sense of critical distance as you obviously have.

As any loyal reader would *really* know, this "witty mind" was born, raised, and educated right here . . . in the *deadlands of Southern California*. Am I happy about that, after thirty-three years? As Melissa Etheridge might say, in an admittedly different context, "Yes, I am!"

I'm aware that being from this *hinterland of the proudly uninformed* is generally considered an attribute too lurid for polite company. Let's face it: Los Angeles is the nation's cultural scapegoat. The rest of you always want—need—to pawn off on us things like David Hasselhoff. I sympathize, but I have news. His would not be a number-one show if only L.A. watched it.

In fact, in a recent visit to Sioux Falls, South Dakota (called by *Fortune* magazine the "number-one city to live in"—L.A., as usual, was buried far below), I was positively pelted with questions about *Baywatch*. To which I say: Wake up, America! Admit it. "We have seen David Hasselhoff, and he is us."

Further, not only am I from this fetid city, I live in its most déclassé part—the San Fernando Valley. Ours is the smoggy grid of tract homes and King Bear Auto Shops you see if you wing north over the crest of the 405. We are Weber Grills, we are doughboy pools cradled in chainlink fence, we are hapless garage sales that amount to no more than a couple of wrinkled "Disco Lady" T-shirts flung out upon a scabrous lawn.

A Chicago colleague once posed to me this analogy: "The San Fernando Valley is to Los Angeles as New Jersey is to New York, right?"

No, it is not. I prefer to think of us as *Long Island with Attitude*. We are the honest middle class finally rising up, taking back what's ours from the smug, incestuous, cultural imperialist hipsters of Manhattan. A smartly self-aware, more-than-meets-the-eye nineties brunette among yesterday's trashy, used-up eighties blondes. We are here and we are America! Even if we don't speak much English. In short, I love the SFV. (To reflect our new image, I propose replacing "San Fernando Valley" with the chic short-hand of "SFV"—much as "Kentucky Fried Chicken" has shifted, subtly, to the taut aerodynamism of "KFC.") I love this grid of mini-malls so blank, so formless, so characterless, because it is my white canvas. Its dull, lidless eye is mine. Its emptiness is my emptiness. Yea, it is my Moby Dick.

So what if I, a cheap nobody, got handed *Buzz*'s "Valley" column only because legend has it that Harlan Ellison was bored by the topic? I cheerfully refuse to be bored by anything. Or I would be out of a job.

As for the light-as-a-$2.99-Chablis title of this book, don't let it fool you. It's not *Depth Takes a Holiday* as in Depth being absent in Los Angeles, a cosmic "Gone Fishing" sign placed upon the work desk where Depth is supposed to be.

No. Think of it more as Depth being tired of, well, of being so darn deep all the time. Depth yearns to don a jaunty Hawaiian shirt and have a hilarious outdoor adventure.

Depth wants a holiday; Depth deserves a holiday. And think about it. Don't you want one, too?

Here: Take this umbrella drink, join me in the pool. We will re-tain our critical distance—I in the shallow end, you in the deep. Our swim will not be a mindless escape, but a profound semiotic act. I think.

Part One

Amongst the Futon-Dwellers

IKEA!
Cry of a
Lost Generation

I will never forget the day I saw my first IKEA home furnishings catalog.

It was early 1991. At the time, I was living in Canoga Park, in a battered house with yellow ocher carpeting and cottage-cheese ceilings that sparkled as gaily as a mirrored ball. That particular day, I was sitting in the living room, among a medley of neo–Salvation Army and marked-down Pier One furniture—pockmarked chairs, chipped lamps, and rickety end tables that faced away from each other as if they were enemies.

I opened the catalog—and in one epiphanic instant, I saw a door swinging wide and a beautiful white light spilling over a land of knotty pine coffee tables with copies of *The Atlantic* scattered on them, leather couches the color of wonderful old saddles, Turkish "Kelim" carpets, blonde bookcases glowing with track lighting, exotic leafy plants nestling in gently glazed terra-cotta pots.

I heard mermaids singing, "Come home! Come home!" Tears stung my eyes. Where had I gone astray?

Because this was my true "inner" living room. It was as "me" as if I had decorated it myself.

It was IKEA-land.

Of course, never in my whole California life had I lived in such a place. My parents, bless their hearts, had been given to things formica, a nonworking fireplace festooned with lawn elves, and nougat-colored couches with giant buckles on them. Now, at twenty-nine, genteel boho poverty had landed me with a passel of male roommates whose chief cultural accomplishment seemed to be an eight-foot-high stack of back issues of the *Los Angeles Times* in our bathroom.

And yet, this dream living room of backlit bookcases, tasteful art, and potted ficuses was utterly familiar to me. I had walked through it often in my mind's eye, during the many hours spent in college dutifully sitting through endless Ingmar Bergman films. Outside would lie a redwood deck overlooking the city, a couple of bottles of white zinfandel, and the piped-in music of—well, damn it anyway—Claude Bolling.

Yes, it was a safe place, a place where one could admit to sometimes feeling less drawn to the Museum of Modern Art than to the museum gift shop to maybe get a Japanese plate with a cat on it. A place where the vague desire to spend years writing some sort of Ann Beattie-ish novel and a yearning to still be able to afford Laura Ashley sheets could meet.

But then came an even more profound revelation.

I realized that until that IKEA catalog hit my doorstep, I had been feeling invisible, undeserving, unattractive, a non-shopper on a consumer planet. What was wrong with me? For a decade, I had been a complete demographic misfit—a victim of Williams-Sonoma tastes on a Pic 'n' Save budget.

I had been slapped around by the likes of Crate & Barrel. Oh, Crate & Barrel, you snow queen of mail-order catalogs, as welcoming as a New England spring breeze—but once inside, your prices turn the bowels to ice: $18.95 for a simple watering can? $69.96 for a bed tray? $199 for a white "French medallion" patio chair (reduced from $349)? My IBM computer isn't worth that much.

And so, in response, I had gone the other way. I had become a consumer self-hater. I spent the entire late eighties shuddering about Los Angeles in a Hyundai Excel without air-conditioning, not caring who knew. I was a dodger of student loans, devoid of dental insurance, a buyer of Payless shoes . . .

Oh my God!

How had this happened?

Consider this story, related recently by a forty-five-year-old woman. It strikes me as a tale that couldn't possibly have been told by a member of "my" generation.

When Don and I were first dating in our twenties, we drove up to Cambria, that little artists' town near Ojai. Stopping at a charming roadside antique store, we saw this old Victorian rocker we both really loved. But it was two hundred dollars! Neither of us had that kind of money.

We drove on, but five miles later we looked at each other

and realized we had to have it. We weren't even living to-gether, mind you—we had only been seeing each other for three weeks, who knew if we were going to last? But darn it if we didn't go back and put in one hundred dollars each. And you know what? We still have that chair today—it's one of our most cherished pieces.

While there is a certain gentle bohemian quality to her story, this is a woman who has never seen the inside of a futon.

And herein lies the generation gap. The idea that I might go halvsies on a $400 Victorian rocker (I adjust for inflation) with a man I had been dating three weeks seems outrageous. Four hun-dred dollars for a one-person object without actual mechanized, moving parts?

As for an antique's "investment" potential, who knows if we're going to be here next week, let alone in ten or twenty years? I can't afford any health insurance, so I'll probably be dead by then. As for having children to pass things on to, where would they stay? It's $800 a month for this lousy two-bedroom apartment.

And there you see the heart of it. Baby Boomers are about per-manence, legacy, and quality. We who came after, on the other hand, are about transience. We can't imagine we'll last the year unless we suddenly win a MacArthur grant or sell a screenplay, in which case we'll have to get all new stuff anyway. We're the people who save a nickel on a parking meter only to get dinged later with an eighteen-dollar ticket.

In fact, we twenty-six- to thirty-two-year-olds are the lost gen-eration.

We're the depressed generation.

We're the disappointed generation.

We're the people that *Time*—or at least *Newsweek*—forgot. Overeducated, underemployed, drowning in student loan payments that will extend past the year 2000, we are "Late Boomers"—that is, those born in the early sixties at the tail end of the Baby Boom.

"Boomers on a Budget" is another descriptive term, but it sounds too cheery, like some kind of bustling Saturday morning PBS do-it-yourself show. "Late Boomer" seems more crestfallen, evocative of having arrived too late for a party.

Which is just how we feel. Only now entering our key power-lunching, German-car-buying years, we're chagrined to have missed the oily treats of the swollen eighties: real-estate speculation, junk bonds, stealing.

We are today's young, highly trained, downwardly mobile professionals: "dumpies." We're just emerging from years of college only to learn that there are no jobs available for people with our advanced qualifications. While we still have yuppie tastes, our *economic* decade is the nineties, a decade no one else wants, a decade in which the silicone implants of the economy have been removed, in which the management pyramid is flattening.

Hitherto, we dumpies have lacked even cultural iconography to rally around. I mean, the flower children had Woodstock. Yuppies had BMWs and Rolexes. What cultural signposts have we Late Boomers enjoyed?

Less Than Zero. The Brat Packers. The film version of *Bright Lights, Big City*, starring Michael J. Fox. Look at the Monaco royals: our parents had Grace Kelly; all we get is Princess Stephanie doing the lambada in a rubber mini-dress.

At a certain point, twenty-something smarminess even became its own sub-genre. A good example is *Bad Influence,* a bad movie currently making cable rounds like an old hooker. Devoid of even one sympathetic character, *Bad Influence* has all the fictional tropes of "our" generation: techno-beat clubs ablaze with pink and turquoise neon; black-clad, arty twenty-three-year-old nymphomaniac girls shifty-eyed with cocaine; clammy-palmed James Spader. The crowning glory, though, is Rob Lowe, post-porn-video-arraignment, flung into the mix like a smelly tennis shoe. He is so "evil" he cannot keep from lifting an eyebrow sardonically every time anyone leaves the room. He even apes a French accent at one point, for reasons I cannot begin to remember.

No wonder we dumpies spent the eighties hiding out in our apartments, watching PBS and eating Trader Joe's pizza. No wonder we were a consumer group in hibernation.

It was in this despair that IKEA founder Ingvar Kamprad detected opportunity.

And in 1991, he came into Southern California, uttering those five immortal words: "Halogen! Impossible Price: $29!" The rest was history.

In that instant, we dumpies found our niche. We rose up and became the IKEA Generation!

In one year, we were to learn the joys of "prosumer"-hood. (In case you didn't know, that's short for "proactive consumer," an enlightened person who understands that self-assembly is the key to furnishing affordability.)

We were to learn how the unique IKEA "flat-packing" technique saves not only millions but the environment, too!

We were to master an exciting new vocabulary. For example, "Billy" bookcases—IKEA's best-selling piece of furniture and therefore, by extrapolation, the best-selling piece of furniture *on the planet.* "Polhem" armchairs. "Larb" end tables . . . actually no, "larb" is a food. I mean "Lack" end tables. ("What they 'lack' is stability," snapped one person whom I did not choose to interview further for this article.) Or how about that handy "Aspvik" sofa bed? (Impossible Price: $179!)

You could, of course, argue that Sweden-based IKEA, purveyor of European-made furnishings at Wal-Mart prices, is merely the world's largest home-furnishings retailer. And you'd be right. With more than one hundred stores in twenty-five countries, IKEA has been celebrated by the *Wall Street Journal,* anointed "Store of the Year" (in 1990) by *Money* magazine. Just last year its U.S. sales alone topped $280 million. (In business since 1943, IKEA even predates STOR, which it bought out last year.)

You could mention that at a time when other major home retailers like RB Furniture are going bankrupt, IKEA has just opened three new stores in Fontana, City of Industry, and Tustin. Or you could talk about the recession—and sure, IKEA's success does reflect the economic downturn that made such reasonably priced retailers as Wal-Mart and Gap last year's merchandising hits.

IKEA's West Coast advertising director, Cynthia Neiman, puts it this way:

We did very well in France, for example, in the early eighties, when Europe was going through a recession. IKEA sort of became a symbol of the smart, economical, practical way to shop. IKEA in Europe was almost sometimes used as an adjective. "It's IKEA-like." Politicians would want to be photographed in front of IKEA furniture in their offices to show how expense-minded they were.

And we really love that image. The whole founding philosophy of the company is to provide quality home furnishings of good form and function at prices so low that the majority of people can afford to buy them. The founder is still alive and very present in the company, and that's still his philosophy.

At IKEA, then, we talk about functional quality. For example, the Billy bookcase. We think a bookcase should be able to hold books—so each shelf in Billy is able to hold fifty pounds of books. It's very sturdy. But the finish on Billy is not water-resistant, like what we would do on a kitchen table, for example. Because we don't think that's a valid function to build into a bookcase—we don't think it's going to be around water!

But all of this is just so much background. The point is, never has a retailer quite gotten so *under the skin* of a generation. What's shocking is that IKEA fits post-boho urban taste so exactly. And so this town is abuzz with small but telling IKEA stories.

Like the thirty-year-old aerospace engineer who stumbled upon an IKEA store back east when visiting friends. Flying into a panic of excitement, she bought eight hundred dollars' worth of IKEA stuff and had it shipped back to L.A. A month later, the Burbank store opened.

Or the twenty-six-year-old Disney production executive who inherited an entire set of IKEA furniture from an actor friend who was leaving the city. He wept when he couldn't disassemble the self-assembled stuff and get it into his Geo.

People even admit privately of IKEA shame. So what, goes the nightmare, if you have a nice "Tulka" loveseat in "Strinne" blue with matched lacquered pine "Ingo" end tables? Everyone knows you paid only five hundred dollars for it! We've all memorized the same fucking catalog! I mean, why buy a BMW when it costs the same as a Hyundai and everyone's driving them?

But remember, we can't afford BMWs. Conspicuous consumption is a thing of the past. Feelings of IKEA shame are flashbacks to the eighties.

Remember that we are dumpies. We don't expect the best. We'll take a smidgen of style at bargain-basement rates.

We are the people who'll take a Hyundai . . . but with a spoiler. Or a Geo Storm: we love its sporty look! So what if its crash-test results are so bad even stunt dummies refuse to get into them?

We can't afford real French Brie—but we'll gladly take Trader Joe's canny invention: *Canadian* Brie! Sure, it's a bit rubbery, but it's cheap and the package *says* Brie.

There are, of course, some Late Boomers who will not buy IKEA. This is a particularly interesting phenomenon, highlighting as it does the fact that where one stands on the IKEA question is, more than any other single indicator, an actual class distinction: it is what separates "Upper" from "Middle" Late Boomers. ("Lower" Late Boomers have never heard of IKEA—or cannot afford even its infamous "As Is" section.)

The fact is, most all Late Boomers are in pretty much the same sad financial boat—an "obscenely extravagant" annual salary of $32,000 not being really so far from your "graduate student stipend" of $13,000 a year. So it is that Upper, Middle, and Lower Late Boomers are distinguished from one another more by differences in attitude than in actual financial standing, those with more discriminating tastes having proportionately more out-of-control Visa bills.

The Middles, or "Wicker Class," are really your main IKEA buyers. The central condition of the Wicker Class is to have both artistic pretensions and an upper-middle-class background. It is this characteristic that accounts for the vague conclusion so prevalent among Middles that one can be an Artist while at the same time never lacking key butcher block items.

At the top of the Middles, you have your actual gainfully employed professionals who simply like the stuff IKEA sells, unaware of any "shame" they should be feeling. More poignant, really, are the "middle" Middles—a sub-group committed to the belief that nine-to-five employment must at all costs be avoided, as it symbolizes a kind of psychic death. This is where you find your part-time community college instructors, your perpetual students floating in and out of graduate programs. They may do scene-painting bouts; they may put in two or three days a week at some horribly banal low-level office job. If they sell a little real estate, they are never successful, being lousy sellers.

Above them are the Upper Late Boomers: less victims of their own creativity, they have flung themselves passionately into the pantyhose-and-tie world. Below are the Lowers, a.k.a. Scary Wanderers Whose Laundry Baskets Overflow. Middles often experience these Lowers as the roommate who can never make his/her rent on time, eking out a life of Ramen as he/she watches Andy Griffith reruns, funded by unemployment and minuscule checks from hostile parents.

Lowers are chiefly used by the other classes as house-sitters, pet-feeders, or furniture-movers. Compensation for such tasks may run five dollars an hour for not more than four hours, a six-pack of Molson, or waiver of a phone bill if appropriate.

A final, special case of the Late Boomer mentality can be seen in a handful of forty-one- to forty-five-year-olds. The operative condition here is essentially ten years lost in graduate school, Oregon, or Paris—or on drugs. While born early enough in the Boom (around 1950) to enjoy the fruit of the Boom, these folks somehow never got quite *with* the Boom. Then the sixties came and they lost their way completely.

Emerging now in the nineties (after the oof has gone out of the Boom), such individuals are experiencing a depressingly late start in everything fiscal. At twenty-five, their parents had their own homes, Christmas Club benefits, and at least three strapping children. At forty-three, it is all some still-unmarried or long-ago divorced Late Boomers can do to keep tiny shards of health insurance alive between employment episodes.

I myself am a classic Middle, with solid Middle tastes. However, as with many other Middles, I'm in the process of slowly being shamed into Upper, even though I can ill afford it. And IKEA, of course, is at the center of that.

Talk about IKEA shame. My boyfriend and I actually bought the dreaded "Ilsbo" couch combination, documented as the rock-bottom cheapest couch or couch-substitute IKEA offers (those foam Aspvik "sofa beds" being the possible exception). This was in mid-1991. By this time, my boyfriend and I had moved from our Canoga Park David Lynch–style living situation into a more socially acceptable Spanish-style house with hard-wood floors. We were redoing our image completely.

In fairness, it must be said that there are many truly nice things in the IKEA catalogue. However, the Ilsbo is not one of them. You know Mr. Ilsbo—a few cushions supported by an unfinished wood frame, watch the splinters. In defense, all we can say is, we were pressed for time: family from South Dakota was getting off the plane in three hours; the stuff was headed outdoors anyway.

But I admit, perhaps I got carried away. It was the come-hither price that did it. Cost for a brand-new matching couch, love seat, and armchair? $434. *$434!* "Ha ha ha ha ha!" I shouted out the window as we trundled down Magnolia Boulevard, the flatbed stacked with IKEA booty. We threw in a four-foot "Ficus Benjamina," a Kelim rug, a $29 halogen torchiere, and somehow the living room almost looked Southwestern, in a rugged sort of way.

Well, the crows would come home to roost three months later. Ah, I remember it well. It was a perfect evening: Miles Davis was playing, people were mingling, no one recognized our Trader Joe's salmon pâté. And then one of our guests, a member of the Industry, lifted a glass of chardonnay to her lips, delivered a witticism about Steve Chao, I think . . . and plunged right through the Ilsbo love seat—with its attractive "Kusta" green pillows—right onto her ass.

Like a bad dog, the entire family Ilsbo was immediately hustled outside.

Okay, it was humiliating. But I went back.

Because the bottom line is, shopping IKEA is a complete, spiritually rejuvenating experience.

Compare, for example, going to Wickes! Surprisingly Wickes!

I cannot tell you what it is, but something about Wickes smells expensive. It is like some giant mini-Hyatt with swooping escalator, big plants, brass pots. At the top of the escalator, a blonde man in a suit, resembling some overearnest USC Business School graduate, appears swiftly at your side. The word *commission* screams hysterically across your mind.

All around is a forest of Italian black leather sofas and tartan taffeta "day beds," business people waiting quietly at oak negotiating desks, "Monthly Payment: Only $170!" stickers dangling everywhere. The bargain-seeking dumpie senses danger.

You can go to Sears, but do you really have nine hundred dollars to spend on a small, pale blue corduroy three-seater with a skirt on the bottom and oak balls on the ends? Do you like ruffles? Do you want something to sit on or to get buried in?

Or do you want to go to one of those "Liquidation! Huge Discounts on Name-Brand Furniture!" places, fluorescently lit warehouses in which recent-immigrant families sadly roam?

Compare that with IKEA!

Gay blue-and-yellow banners out on the boulevard herald your arrival, as if to some world's fair. Enormous signs tell you where to park, where to walk, where to load: one half expects to see a monorail whizzing up above.

In the IKEA foyer, you are seized with a feeling of indescribable happiness. The general feeling—of bright colors, big windows, educational displays—is of having entered some marvelous Montessori-type school for creatively gifted children. (For some of us, being named a "gifted child" was the last happy time we can remember, before endless adult temp experiences disappointed.)

On your left are some enormous metal bins with bright yellow carrier-bags in them. Pencils are also provided. To your right is the "ball room," a glassed-in room full of colorful balls! In fact, it is for one's children. You can sign them in and leave them there for hours. Just ahead is the "diaper room."

A wave of liberal emotion sweeps over you. Good God— American *corporations* cannot even provide on-site child care for families and mothers. And here is IKEA, a home-furnishing store, bending over backward to provide free diapers. Surely on-site, IKEA-sponsored medical care cannot be far behind.

Across from the diaper room is a quasi-scientific exhibit of more clever "child-proofing" doodads than one could ever imagine. But underneath is the kicker. Image after image has been piling up, but what takes the vision of a whole New Democratic Order over the top is a shiny, brand-new Volvo with a big bow on top.

Of course. Scandinavian ingenuity. Safety meeting design; the Volvo; the very sanctuary of the modern family. Atop the car—

under the bow—sits a special removable IKEA luggage rack with which you can haul your furniture home. Price: twenty-two dollars. (Needless to say, a full refund will be cheerfully given upon the rack's safe return to mother ship IKEA.)

Because IKEA is the mother ship; IKEA is a mother, a good mother, whose white pine and goose-down comforters sing the song of Sweden! IKEA stands for incredible human goodness, of a certain long-forgotten standard of Western morality. The Italians have had their ugly moments, and God knows the Germans have, but never the Swedes! The Swedes are a neutral people, a fair people, a moral people!

It is all we can do not to throw ourselves down on the floor and bow before the image of the slightly balding Ingvar Kamprad. Not so much a nerdy dweeb as, really, an honest guy from the little town of Älmhult who sold matchbooks and had a simple dream . . .

"To create a better everyday life for the majority of people."

How many Republican politicians can say they've done that? How many *Democrats*?

Ethan Allen (antique*like* retail furniture) has recently begun running some very daring, semiotically loaded TV spots. To Wave-type jazz, casual camera shots show a hip urban couple, right around thirty, redecorating their apartment.

Out go the white cube end tables, the cheerful yellow cloth chairs, a Scandinavian-type sofa bed, the blonde wood bookshelves laden with beloved but painfully dog-eared paperbacks. In come an antique clock, a heavy oak dining table, Duncan Phyfe-esque chairs.

"When you're ready for real furniture . . ." a narrator says—not condescendingly, but definitely weighing his words. "At Ethan Allen, you can buy antiques without a lot of money."

Well, let us know when the economy bounces back and gives us another chance at an economically comfortable adulthood. Maybe then we'll think about relinquishing our Billy bookcases.

But until then, we'll help ourselves to another slice of Canadian Brie, thank you.

The
Joy of
Temping

Nowadays when I hit the light at Burbank and Laurel Canyon, I get to turn my car south. Yes, south—toward Studio City, West Hollywood, and Beverly Hills—because I have meetings now, I do. My career has progressed to the point where I actually get to meet with Industry people and brainstorm plot twists for movies-of-the-week. After two years of these meetings, all I've gotten out of them are a handful of dry Chinese-chicken-salad lunches and parking validation (most of the time), but that's another story.

The point is, I'm grateful to be in a loop, any loop, even a rotten loop. Because a couple of years ago, I used to go north on Laurel Canyon. North. Deep into Van Nuys, North Hollywood, and Sylmar: land of fluorescent lighting, faux hardwood paneling, olive-green carpet, and gummy IBM Selectrics.

I went north because I was a temp. That is, I was a W2-form-carrying member of Stivers Temporary Personnel (Executive & Legal Secretaries, Clerks, Word Processors, Receptionists, Data

Entry). You haven't seen America until you've temped your way across the floor of the San Fernando Valley.

My story begins in early 1990, a bad year. A year in which I was trying to do nothing but write. After three months, my daily routine had dwindled to waiting for form rejection letters to flutter in through the mail slot. Uncontrollable weeping would follow, then the ritual, Medea-like howling of my mantra: "I'm a failure! I'm a failure!" The rest of my time was spent gaining thirteen pounds, refusing to change out of my sweats outfit, and accusing my live-in boyfriend of not finding me attractive anymore.

God has a way of making you run out of money at certain moments in your life—his way, I guess, of making you say *uncle*. And so it was that my fingers ended up walking through the Yellow Pages and landing on Stivers Temporary Personnel.

It was a cold day in February when I drove to Ventura Boulevard for my personal-skills evaluation. And yet, waiting at a stoplight, I had to admit it felt pretty good to be out of the house, showered and dressed, doing something. It was heartening to imagine buying groceries again—Wheat Thins, shampoo, maybe even some Gallo wine (French Colombard, $4.29 a jug!). Even better, it immediately became clear that the good folks at Stivers were going to release me from the terrible burden of being myself. No one asked difficult questions, like, "At age twenty-eight, with a B.S. in physics and two master's degrees, shouldn't you be making more than $7.75 an hour?" On the contrary, they asked, "Can you type?"

And amazingly, I could. Sixty words—count 'em, sixty—a minute. There were pleased smiles all around. I felt a surge of confidence. So what if these weren't words that *Vanity Fair* would even care to glance through? The talent liaisons assured me my efforts were worth something, particularly since there were minimal spelling errors and I'd tabbed over correctly.

In fact, I was feeling a kind of temp euphoria reported by many other unemployed bohemians. Maybe we couldn't finish that Ph.D. thesis/novel/screenplay about the Korean War/found-object earring collection/relationship/grant proposal/tuba symphony/ (your own gnawing onus here), but think how many things we *can* do, and do very well: alphabetize, change paper trays, weigh mail, make coffee. And, of course, nothing spells satisfaction like filched office supplies.

My first temp job was, believe it or not, for a magician. A magician! He was a mild-mannered fellow who had a small, shabby office in North Hollywood, right off Lankershim. Or, I should say, off-off Lankershim. It was in one of those quasi-industrial alleys where they sell things like steel cable, bolts, and pliers.

In my mind, magicians were Seigfried and Roy or nothing. Who knew there was anything in between? But indeed, this man—whom I had never heard of—was working, even touring: Reno, cruise ships, dinner theater in Salinas. This man's phone was ringing.

My job was to type "show lists" like mini-haiku:

Linking rings
Three scarves
Girl in box (use audience member)
End with monkey

You want glamor? From North Hollywood, I traveled north to an amp factory in Sylmar. Don't laugh: this was the prince of gigs. Not only was I pulling in a whopping eleven dollars an hour, but my boss had only one rule: "Absolutely no beer before four P.M." And, as if that weren't enough, this was the job that made me part of publishing history. Have you ever been in an amplifier store and seen *The Tube Amp Book II,* by R. Aspen Pittman? I typed that!

Of course, it wasn't long before my feelings of temp euphoria came crashing down to earth. It happened at Kramer-Wilson Insurance Company in North Hollywood. . . .

Let's begin by considering the phrase *statistical typing pool.* Can you think of anything less statistical than twenty hostile women being paid $8.75 an hour to type numbers onto triplicate insurance forms from eight A.M. to five P.M.? Especially since nowadays any five-hundred-dollar Radio Shack computer can do this job more quickly and efficiently, and without having to go to the bathroom to adjust its slip every fifteen minutes.

But somehow the nineties had not reached Kramer-Wilson. For that matter, neither had the sixties. Because, to add insult to injury, Kramer-Wilson felt that ours was a task that could not be performed without control-top pantyhose. At least that's what our manager, a sixtyish, birdlike woman named Frances, maintained. Every morning she'd walk up and down the aisles of typists, silently patrolling. After lunch (Carl's Jr.), violators of the pantyhose law would receive their reprimand.

My third reprimand occurred on a day when I was wearing pants, boots, and knee socks (plus a turtleneck sweater, bra, clean underwear, and a Daisy-Fresh panty shield, if you must know).

Not an inch of leg or arm was showing. I reeked of Dial. And yet, Frances assured me in hushed tones, without pantyhose I was in violation. Something about health codes. My face went red.

My friend Mel suggested I should have pulled Frances aside and whispered, "I *am* wearing pantyhose, but I had to cut out the crotch ventilator panel, and here it is."

Of course, I didn't think to do that at the time. I returned to the typing pool and realized that the mail boy had come early, wheeling off a whole sheaf of car-insurance premium statements upon which I had typed $3,000 instead of $300. I had intended to open them all and fix my mistake—but why? The error wouldn't be discovered for another week; by then, I'd be history. Like the many unnamed who had gone before me, I had uncovered the power of being a temp.

At 3:15 P.M. all the typists retired, as we did every day, to the snack room for a fifteen-minute break. There, under the hum of fluorescent lights, vending machines gently cradled shiny packets of Doritos, Cheez Doodles, and Chips Ahoy! cookies. Red digital letters flashed ENJOY A TASTY SNACK TREAT NOW . . . ENJOY A TASTY SNACK TREAT NOW . . . And that day, dammit, I did.

Woman's Day
Speaker

When I was invited to perform for Women's History Week at Venice High School, I was excited.

In my mind's eye, I pictured an intimate audience of the already way converted: pensive sixteen-year-old girls with frizzy hair and Birkenstocks, and their rapt English teachers, who would not ever interrupt me except perhaps once, to ask some admiring question like the one I'd been asked the week before on a Feminist Experimental Music radio show:

> Most women composers are vocalists. Is that because the woman's body is like . . . a Vessel . . . which contains . . . the Voice?

Afterward I'd lead them in a few chants—"Women, unite!" "Our bodies, ourselves!"—collect my check, and go home.

I was looking forward to Women's History Week as a kind of

sisterly haven away from the harsh and uncaring audiences that artists sometimes face.

The Venice High School auditorium was a large echoing place with American flags drooping on both sides of the proscenium. At a quarter to twelve, the doors opened and, flanked by their grim instructors, over seven hundred kids of wildly divergent ethnicities came piling in. Although in fact they were oddly unified—white, black, Asian, Latino—all wore the regulation buzz haircuts, baggy pants, and $120 running shoes required by MTV.

Too late I realized that Venice High School's lunch hour (the sun shone brightly outside, gulls wheeled, flags waved) had been axed to make way for this mandatory, hour-long assembly. Women's History Week had shrunk to Women's History Hour, due to a budget crisis, and I . . . was the "star."

"Welcome, Venice High School!" It was Francine Barnett, the woman who had hired me, at the podium. Francine Barnett, whom I now saw as the befuddled, hopelessly-out-of-touch-with-the-nineties-white-liberal-from-Topanga-in-a-Laura-Ashley-dress that she really was.

"Welcome, Venice High Schoolers, to Women's History Week!"

Jeers, boos, catcalls. My stomach turned to ice. Paper cups, Burger King debris were being hurled toward the podium. I was shocked by the candor of their hostility.

Francine's cheeks blushed red for a moment, but she plunged bravely forward, a woman on a mission, the sort of teacher that inspiring ABC Afterschool Specials will later be made about. "I know you may feel that way now," she said, "but after you hear

our speaker present today, an actress from the community . . .
Sandra Loch . . . I know you'll be completely won over.

"But first," she continued, "we'd like to show you this inspiring ten-minute film which I think really sets the tone for what Women's History Week is all about."

Momentarily lulled by curiosity, like an enormous monster whose evening snack is insisting upon doing a jolly little jig before being devoured, the crowd settled somewhat as the lights dimmed.

The film projector was one of those clattering contraptions one finds only in high schools; after much shaking and wild, darting readjustments, a flickering picture appeared on the screen. It was a circa 1971 feminist montage (with 1971 fashions) of a long-haired Joni Mitchell–type woman riding bareback in the desert; of a perky brunette in construction helmet, with drill; of a bespectacled school teacher; of a white-coated female doctor with clipboard, bun, stethoscope. . . .

"She's a child . . . of the de-e-sert," some unnamed folksinger sang, the sound warbling badly. "She's a child of the sea. . . ."

A howl rose up from the mob, so piercing it was like an arrow. After a momentary confusion, and much excited murmuring among the teachers, the lights snapped on and a small, stout, mean-looking woman shot forward to the podium. She was apparently "the heavy."

"Gondoliers!" she hissed. (The "Gondolier" was apparently the school mascot—so that's what the students were called.) "Gondoliers! We've worked very hard to give you this Women's History Week presentation! You want to leave? You want to leave?" Her eyes glinted triumphantly behind round spectacles. "Go ahead! Your teachers will take your names as you leave for detention next week!"

That gave the mob momentary pause. After a small, tight silence, the lights went down and the clattering film started up once more: "She's a child . . . of the de-e-sert!"

I do not remember anything about my performance except that I shot through forty-five minutes of material in under sixteen.

"And now, welcome your classmate Keiko Johnston," I heard as I stumbled out to the wings to the barest smattering of applause. Looking over my shoulder, I saw a thin, angry, pimply sixteen-year-old girl—hair over the face, a "Cure" T-shirt, black jeans. She was carrying what appeared to be a dog-eared poetry journal.

She lifted it and read:

Mirror
Broken glass
Who am I?
Who am I really?
Shards of pain
You don't understand

There was a sharp intake of breath. The words sank in. And then slowly, tumultuously, the applause began, the shouting, the cheering: "Roof, roof, roof, roof!" And then in a trancelike way, the chants began: "Kei-ko! Kei-ko! Kei-ko! Kei-ko!" She was the bard of their generation!

The young thug whose job it was to open and close the curtains at that moment turned to me and said—not maliciously, but with a kind of pitying fairness: "Oh, yeah. Keiko Johnston. I know her. We have Driver's Ed together. She played piano in the Talent Show. *Stairway to Heaven*. Now *there* is someone with real talent."

Nudes
on Ice

When Mike first told me he was going to Las Vegas for two weeks to do the Marilyn McCoo, show at the Desert Inn, I was excited.

Two weeks in Las Vegas! Marilyn McCoo, with her big hair and rhinestone gowns, singing "Up, Up and Away," stretch limousines, free cocktails, shrimp in a glass, showgirls popping amyls!

Mike and I would be put up in some hideous but impossibly luxurious high-rise hotel with a swim-up bar. I would sit on the balcony in dark sunglasses every day, the ruthless desert sun beating down as I typed on and on about the human decay surrounding me. Some incredible novel would emerge—or at least a searing *Rolling Stone* article of some kind.

It would be Hunter S. Thompson-esque. Mike and I would drink tequila in the bathtub, screaming with laughter, saying brilliant things about America and how it was all collapsing. We would smoke pot and have sex all the time.

The first problem was the hotel. Room 347 of the Mardi Gras

Inn boasted only Sanyo toaster oven, faulty air-conditioning, and staticky HBO. Worn beige carpet and a chipped toilet seat completed the picture. Children howled from the pool area.

The second was that, unlike Hunter S. Thompson et al., Mike had a work schedule. It turned out to be from about four in the afternoon until two in the morning, six nights a week. I stayed in bed drinking wine coolers in his absence, watching television, not typing a word.

Upon his return, finally, we would share a bag of Doritos and watch some late-night HBO Jacuzzi movie (*The Hot Tub Club* or *Death Spa*), sadly waiting for the odd exposed breast to bubble toward the screen. Then we'd drop off into fitful sleep while the air conditioner shuddered and moaned.

This wasn't the Vegas I'd envisioned.

But on the fifth day: oil. Or so I thought.

Flipping through the *Vegas Visitor* in my Seagram's-induced torpor, buckets of chicken wings around me as I sat up in bed, I suddenly saw it, the show to end all shows. Its title was three small words, harmless when taken individually and yet volatile in their great and terrible new juxtaposition:

"NUDES ON ICE!"

I lay back, hyperventilating. "The horror, the horror," I whispered excitedly, Brando-esque.

"NUDES ON ICE!" The words bore into my brain. What person could have come up with such a concept? It was the pinnacle of vulgarity—no, it was beyond vulgarity, in that it was the perfect expression of it, and once that concept was expressed, the object itself disappeared and there was only its perfect image.

Nude blonde women . . . in big Las Vegas Lido hats . . . on ice skates. As *dinner theater*.

Were I to venture to that place, to that "NUDES ON ICE!" place, I would stand at the mystical edge of the universe, dark clouds bleeding across a troubled sky, the ocean churning below. I would stand at the very nadir of the human psyche.

"Ah—yes." I was on the phone. "I'm sure you don't have any tickets to tonight's early show at the Union Plaza Hotel?"

I figured such a high-concept show—the nudes, the ice—must be sold out for weeks, the people clawing, screaming to get in.

I heard the clicking of a computer keyboard. "Oh, you mean 'Nudes on Ice'?" the girl asked blandly.

"'Nudes on Ice,' yes," I replied, wanting the girl to know that I was not afraid of saying it.

"Oh, yeah. Still plenty of tickets. How many?" the girl continued, without comment.

"One."

"Visa or MasterCard number?" In growing amazement, I realized that apparently this was nothing more than some quotidian ritual to this girl. One could buy one or a hundred tickets to "NUDES ON ICE!" and she was not going to involve you in any kind of dialogue along the way!

Now maybe if I were a man, this would make sense: putting the ice-skating shows of naked women on credit cards was something one expected men to do—they were forever shocking one with revelations about the topless dancers they had once dated, etc.

But here *I* was—a lone woman—treating myself on a weeknight to "NUDES ON ICE!" Didn't that seem a little strange? What possible dark occasion could I be celebrating?

This question still haunted me as I entered the lobby of the Union Plaza Hotel, a sea of noise and bright lights and slot machines jingling.

Unsure of what single women wore to nude shows—not to mention nude *ice-skating* shows—I had opted for strict business dress. Shoulder pads, a skirt. I jotted notes on a clipboard as I moved forward. If anyone asked me what I was doing there, I would say, "I'm in Quality Control," or something to the effect.

But even as I took my seat of shame within the "NUDES ON ICE!" theater, I could tell that formalities were being dispensed with, and rapidly.

For one thing, the theater was shockingly small and dingy. Flanked by worn red velvet curtains, it exuded not unbridled debauchery, but rather that sort of brave jollity you see in some of the less popular children's attractions at Disneyland. The stage, hidden behind a wrinkled curtain, looked much too tiny to house an ice rink of the stunning proportions I had imagined.

And the audience! Rather than swank cokeheads wearing chinchilla coats, diamond ankle bracelets, and nothing else, they were mostly nice-looking fortyish couples from the Midwest—the women in slacks, the men in feedstore caps.

Even more humiliating: it wasn't a full house.

The lights dimmed. From a little booth up above, a miserable little pit band of six musicians with thinning hair and cheap tuxedos (the hunched violinist; the small bald man with big discolored kettle drums) broke tinnily into the *New York, New York* theme.

As the drums rolled, an announcer gaily introduced "NUDES ON ICE!" . . . *by saying who was in it*. And to my horror, it appeared as though its participants boasted actual skating credentials. It was so unutterably dark—apparently, one of tonight's Nudes had actually won the Olympic Bronze medal in Helsinki!

The curtain lifted. We strained forward.

There was the swirl of rhinestones and pink feathers: a dozen smiling women with big eyebrows and plumed headdresses skated about on the tiny stage before a gaily painted backdrop that looked like some hideous flat out of *Hee-Haw*. But where were the Nudes?

And then you realized: at both sides of the stage, two skaters were standing, frozen, like ornamental urns. Their big plumed headdresses pushed down on their foreheads. Their bedraggled pink feathers seemed sorely in need of dry cleaning.

While they were not strictly nude, a piece of material that usually covered the bust seemed to be missing. They were the Nudes, and they were none too pleased about it.

And all about them, as if in a bejeweled kaleidoscope, the others who had material across the tops of their costumes skated about merrily, doing lazy turns, shaking their feathers out, free of the Burdens of the Nude. From the right and the left, the two Nudes scowled on.

Lost in
CD-ROM
Land

The information superhighway is broad and fast and power-ful. So much so that even I got swept up by it. That's how big this new interactive/CD-ROM/multimedia/edutainment/what-ever thing is!

My story begins three months ago. There I sat, at home in my sweatpants, ankle-deep in my thirties, depressed. I was a brilliant iconoclast with multiple college degrees, a richly eclectic back-ground, and a host of unique, hard-to-categorize, creative skills. In short, I was unemployed.

That changed in one phone call. My friend Max from college needed an assistant producer on a new educational CD-ROM for kids called *Meet the Mammals!* There would be pay.

I flew into a flurry of excitement. I wanted to know all. Why *Meet the Mammals!*? Because mammals are popular in the very key five-to-eight-year-old age range. What were CD-ROMs again? Living books with film, narration, and music. Whom would I be working for? KidSmart, Inc., a Glendale multimedia firm. Though small (fewer than a hundred employees), it was replicating like a virus. Investors were hurling cash at it by the fistful.

Max's budget? Two hundred fifty thousand dollars. I could hardly believe it. The media "projects" we'd worked on together in the past had cost in the low three digits and depended heavily on the uncompensated services of hostile work/study students from Pomona.

Special skills needed? None! Max already had five computer programmers so smart they could invent a new language and destroy it in the same day if they had a mind to. My tasks? Keeping all these skilled, clever people connected, stocking the fridge with Mountain Dew, looking at a computer screen occasionally, and saying vague things like, "This corner over here needs more red, I think. Then again, I'm not really an artist. You do what you want."

My first day at KidSmart, Inc., was so exciting I thought I'd faint. Inside the blank modern mini-mall where the company was housed, you could feel the roar, the heat of the info superhighway, with all of its tremendous "baud." Row after row of genius-level twenty-somethings were packed into cubicles stabbing at keyboards as rocket ships and pterodactyls and numerals flew across their screens while strange chirpy children's voices sang: "WEL-come to THE Kids-o-TOR-ium!"

I, by contrast, was given some light typing. Invoices, I think they called them. However, soon I, too, was led to a fast, gleaming computer—a Pentium. Such a great word. Like some grim disciplinary tool of the future: "Sandra, get back to your Pentium!" Shoulder to shoulder with the rest, I plunged into the digital maw. C-prompt. W-I-N. Boom. I was in. I was one of them!

At noon, trays of spaghetti, garlic bread, and chocolate chip cookies were flung onto hallway tables. Electronic warriors all, we fell on the grub like wild dogs. This ritual persisted daily. Apparently, it was cheaper for KidSmart, Inc., to swell our bodies with fatty foods than lose our brains for an hour while we bumbled off to lunch. *That's* how fast this industry is moving.

Then again, where is it moving to?

Weeks later the *Meet the Mammals!* project was coming to a triumphant close. I myself had contributed a few jaunty mammal puns, the bold idea that our "help" icons should be more of a turquoise and less of a teal, and what is known as "compressing the piss" out of the sound—shrinking the music data from a rich, lifelike 16 bits, 44100 Hz., to a small, tinny 8 bits, 11025 Hz.

Then the darkness began to fall. Our next project? A choice between *Meet the Fish!*, *Meet the Dinosaurs!*, *Meet the Birds!*, or perhaps the edgier *Meet the Sharks!*

I felt a pang of disappointment as I hunched over my Pentium. All around me, the programmers in their jeans and wrinkled T-shirts continued to stab at keyboards. Soon the ritual fatty foods would be flung out. For the one thousandth time the strange chirpy children sang:

"WEL-come to THE Kids-o-TOR-ium!"

It was just that . . . I'd been told interactive CD-ROM technology was the wave of the future. A whole new kind of entertainment—of art, even—would be possible! We'd be thinking in four dimensions, deconstructing our own novels, bringing world peace by modem in ten different time zones at once. Not *Meet the Fish!*

But then I realized it: tomorrow's computer technology is not for us adults. It can't be. Look at us.

I, for one, cannot physically handle any more computer stimulation. After just three months of working sixty hours a week at KidSmart, Inc., I'm already developing the trademark ailments of the cyber-generation: bad eyesight, carpal tunnel syndrome, greenish skin. I can barely make it from computer to car without a limp. Yesterday I saw the profile of James Cagney in my cellulite.

Even the twenty-year-olds at KidSmart, Inc., are wasting away. One quality tester I saw last week had gray teeth. His gums also were not looking their best. How does this happen?

Where can we find new humans upon which this relentlessly burgeoning new CD-ROM technology host can suck and feed? We must turn to our country's very young. The children. And nothing will do but the very best children: the Baby Boomer children. They still have their eyesight; their fingers are still nimble; their cheeks are still soft and rosy; their trust funds are bulging.

I have seen these kids. They come to KidSmart, Inc., on-site tours to demo our nauseatingly top-quality products. They are being groomed by their dads (JPL engineers with a wee bit too much time on their hands) to vanquish and possibly eat other children by virtue of the superior hyper-learning they begin at a disgustingly young age.

How? Through CD-ROMs that we pack with secret anagrams hidden in flying pterodactyls and laughing flowers and odd, terrible songs that improve math skills to an awful degree. Songs like . . .

"WEL-come to THE Kids-o-TOR-ium!"

This is why when night falls we play a round of networked Doom—an ultraviolent computer game. Basically, you run behind a big gun and shoot everything in sight. Or you may take the chainsaw. We use the special hacker "Barney" patch. All at once a purple dinosaur is lumbering heavily after you, wailing, "I love you, you love me!" But he hurls green fireballs; his love is not for us.

These Little Town Blues

These days, it doesn't take much—a leaf falling outside my window, an old Dave Brubeck tune wafting over the radio—to make me realize how much I miss New York.

Not that I've ever lived there. No. Couldn't find my way from West 51st Street to East 52nd (assuming such addresses even exist) if you paid me.

But I should have lived there. More important, I should have done so in my twenties, when I still had the energy and the wits to survive in such a place. (With wobbling hands, I slosh more Gallo French Colombard into my glass, cutting it with a careless dash of Diet 7-Up.) Most of my twenties were spent in Pasadena, which, admittedly, proved quite convenient in terms of grocery shopping. ("Convenient grocery shopping." You see? That's what I hate about myself! I would never make it in New York. I'm just not tough enough. I suck!)

Now, at age thirty-one—a sort of demographic nowhere land between *Glamour* and *Lear's*—such thrilling adventures are forever lost to me. Remorse has come to visit me like a grieving friend. The laughter has died from my face; my strapless party dress is looking a bit poochy around the middle; my hair, which was piled up on my head in a twisty, festive Claudia Schiffer top-knot is beginning to wilt, tendril by tendril. I keep looking around anxiously for the rest of my twenties, turning my beaded black purse upside down and shaking it, but there does not seem to be anything left. Uh-oh.

The main thing I realize, now that I'm ankle-deep in my thirties and my health insurance premiums are rising, is that I led my life totally backward. (Note how I speak in the past tense now. Henceforth, I shall be looking only backward, my every waking second tinged with regret. Granted, I may tire of this when I hit forty and realize I still have another forty healthy-as-a-horse years to go. But I figure I'll cross that bridge when I come to it.)

I should have lived in New York, *then* L.A. Of course, I never thought about such things in my twenties. I was too busy . . . sleeping.

I can recall some mornings sleeping until eleven. What the hell was I thinking? Occasionally some sort of sexual activity was involved, yes. Sounds terrific—but on second thought, how good was it?

Not very.

Truly, if you collected all the men I slept with in my twenties in one group, say at some Van Nuys Holiday Inn, in some sort of hideous alumni event, it would be sad indeed. It would be a comparatively small group, of course. Most would be trying to dodge the modestly priced $15 admission fee, shuffling about in their rumpled crewnecks, pleading car trouble.

Perhaps I sound a bit crabby, a bit harridanlike. Fine. I grant you that. I just feel that maybe I paid for a few too many of my own meals in my twenties. (Theirs, too!) I'm remembering a lot of gamey Cobb salads, hard-as-a-rock sourdough rolls, and lone glasses of watery Chablis. Of El Torito happy hours, I've had a few. Oh, my stomach twists in fury. What of the fabulous dates twenty-five-year-olds always have? Wasn't I supposed to have been flown in a private plane to . . . to San Francisco at least? For dinner and the opera? Simply because I was twenty-five?

Oh, why didn't I spend my twenties in New York like everyone told me to? Think how different this all would have been. First of all, I would have looked fa-a-abulous. The unending heat in Los Angeles, bringing with it in a damp, lowering cloud a fatal monsoon of saggy tube tops, drawstring terry-cloth shorts, and plastic flip-flops bought as a quick afterthought at Thrifty Jr., has been the death of me. I apologize to anyone who saw me and my puffy toes—and everything else—in my twenties. It was just that I was so hot! So miserable!

Let's face it, for half of my twenties not even my dressy outfits were working. Not that they are working today, but at least the timber makes a softer crash when it falls. Older and wiser, I know my limits. I no longer try for things I can't pull off. Don't press me for details. The only phrase I will utter is *cowboy epaulets*. I don't want to go into it any further than that. Oh, all right. *Rubber pants*. I've said it. I am humiliated.

Compare that with my life in New York (that I never led).

Don't I look wonderful? There I am, an eternal twenty-six years old, rushing about in the crisp winter air with flushed cheeks, striking in some sort of full-length black wool coat accessorized with a bright red muffler. What is it that I have tucked under my arm? Could that be . . . a novel of some sort? Why, yes! It's the novel (or play, opera, book of stunning poems, Ph.D. thesis) I wrote between seven and eleven A.M.—when some people in Los Angeles were sleeping. Sleeping! In their terry-cloth shorts with their puffy toes.

Shhh! Wait. What is that exciting person with her dark hair in her striking black winter coat and bright red muffler doing now? Why, she's jumping into a cab and heading up 57th, down 43rd, up 111th, and down 13th. How thrilling! It's a career in itself. (Just the fact that all New York streets seem to be numbers excites me. Compare with: up Reseda, down Vanowen, right on Kester, left on Victory, and there you are in the parking lot of the Van Nuys Lucky.)

I alight from the cab in front of the elegant brownstone I share with some subtly wealthy older but handsome man named Hans who is this century's great genius of . . . I don't know—painting, the theater, whatever. OK, photography. Good. I will live with him for three years before striking out boldly on my own, sucking his key contacts along with me. At that point I will trade him for a much younger person—a hotheaded bisexual sculptor named Frank, or at least a sloe-eyed bulimic named Ondine.

For now, Hans and I live in an exciting, exotic hub where Gordon Lish is perpetually dropping by—too often sometimes—as he finds my pesto amusing. Meanwhile, Hans is working on a destined-to-become-famous photo-collage of me called *saNDrA*.

Remember that I am twenty-six and faultless, at least in my winter coat with muffler and boots and mittens and a red cloche hat. *saNDrA* ends up at the Whitney coinciding with the publication of my novel about how difficult it is to live in New York, how chilling the winters, how inconvenient the grocery shopping.

The Best Opening Lines for L.A. Women: Based on Their Iconic Earrings

It's Saturday night in the mid-Wilshire area, and you are crammed into someone's kitchen swilling white wine with laughing arty people, none of whom you know. You don't even remember who invited you here, but the joint is jumping and a cursory glance tells you the crowd is hip—there are *L.A. Style* magazines lying around and a fifties-era dinette in the kitchen; Cole Porter music is on; angel-hair pasta is out; plastic dinosaurs spar behind ferns in the bathroom. There is the correct percentage of black clothing here and of men in ponytails, as well as the two requisite bored-looking, obscenely underage girls in black lingerie and spectacularly botched hair-dye jobs who don't mingle with anyone and eventually leave early.

Are these magazine people? Are they art people? Are they art people with a leg up in the film industry? Is there a drug dealer in back? Will famous people show up? If they do, should you ignore them? How many plates of pasta can you have before it starts looking uncool? Are those sleazy Hollywood people in the corner wearing torn leather as a fashion statement, or are they actually penniless? Can you leave your eighty-five-dollar sweater on this chair, or will someone take it?

We can't answer all of those questions, but we can give you tips on how to pick up—or at least talk to—a woman. The potential for meaningful repartee will be maximized if you begin by correctly reading her earrings, which she will no doubt emphatically shake at you when she talks. Women in Los Angeles are hanging anything on their ears these days—from little beaded facsimiles of Hopi Indian shields to Campbell's soup cans. Social earwear in Los Angeles has evolved into a rigorously coded identification not only of tribe—the Industry tribe, the postmodern tribe, the tribe who want to give out their phone numbers tonight no matter what—but of mood, of sexual tastes, of the statement she may wish to make this evening on the work of art in the age of mechanical reproduction. . . .

1. Simple Gold Studs:

There are two possibilities:

1. This woman, at age twenty-five, has just had her ears pierced for the first time. She has to keep these studs in for six weeks, turning them and putting alcohol on them every day. The woman at Bojangles swore that if she hung stuff in them prema-

turely, she would get these huge slits in her ears. This is kind of a "down time" for her socially. Leave her alone.

2. This woman has been wearing astonishing, very heavy earrings recently and screwing them down way too hard. She's probably in a high-tension field—film production, maybe, the business aspect, anyway, some career where it is necessary to sweep into lunch meetings at the Columbia Bar and Grill with enormous geometric earrings, four-inch heels, and shoulder pads swollen to the brink of parody. Now she has an infection. So the studs are in—who cares? She didn't expect to run into anyone here she knows. She has calls to make in the morning. She's just here tonight as a favor to the host. She plans to leave by eleven. There's a lot of unresolved tension here, which could suddenly become sexual if you seize the moment and say something that totally confuses her. "I'd like to rip off your panties and wear them on my head like a hat" would be an arresting opener, for instance.

2. Two Simple Gold Studs in Each Ear:

This woman doesn't want to hit you over the head with it, but she is open to new experiences. She's a discreet woman in a period of experimentation. She asked the leaf-blower man in the other day—for coffee, that's all. They talked about novels. Turns out he was an English major for two years before dropping out of college. He loved Dickens but didn't see where it all was going career-wise. She has always toyed with the idea of having a Jacuzzi put in, and apparently he knows how to do that, too. He gave her his card.

"How old are you? Really? How old?" Confronting this woman and delivering this bombshell will instantly snap her to attention. While many women will simply pick up their drinks and move elsewhere, this one will narrow her eyes and settle in for a series of seductive and snappy quips. "Well, how old do you think I am? Why is age important? How old are you that you would ask that question?"

3. Seven Simple Gold Studs in Each Ear:

Obviously into pain. This woman, probably young, is guaranteed to have the most spectacularly nihilistic day job you have ever heard of, like cleaning toilets at the Greyhound bus station. Of all the dingy minimum-wage jobs available—boxing groceries, delivering medical supplies—this person went out of her way to find one that has the desired annihilating effect. This person reads her own poetry real late at the Anti-Club. If you really feel up to it, take a bite into a cracker with cheese, let it fall onto the floor, and then say dully, "I hate this kind of cheese—it smells like shit." Wait for a rejoinder. If none comes within ten minutes, best move on.

4. Gold Hoops:

a) Gold Hoops the Diameter of Quarters:

This woman is a co-worker at someone's day job—the bank, perhaps—and is strictly along for the ride. This is not exactly like an office party, but she's glad to be out. She can handle whatever comes along. Almost anything makes a decent opening: "Is that salsa any good?" "God, it's warm in here!" "Are there any more cups in that bag?"

b) Gold Hoops the Diameter of Grapefruits:

Big, big, big! This is probably the hostess. She needed some short, telegraphic way of indicating, among all these vibrant women, that she is the hostess. Don't try to pick up the hostess.

5. Bananas, Apples, Cherries, Oranges:

A woman wearing gaudy simulacra of fruit in her ears should be handled with caution. A clock is ticking here, almost audibly. She seems to be funny, enthusiastic, girlish—what you don't see is the deadly panic that has set in ever since she looked into the mirror one morning and saw crow's feet starting around her eyes. Can it be that she is *no longer nineteen?* What has she done with her life, and where is she going? Why is her car making that funny sound? Where is the incredible man who was supposed to walk into her life before she turned thirty? Help! The result has been a fury of activity: She has started aerobics again, joined Great Expectations and enrolled in a screenwriting class at UCLA Extension, and plans to explore tantric yoga immediately. This woman may seem giddily optimistic, but she does not have time to waste. "Will you marry me now?" is an acceptable opening line.

6. Sea Gull Feathers, Odd-Shaped Rocks You Can't Quite Identify:

There is definitely a Topanga thing happening here, in which case this woman is lost at this party. These simply aren't her people. She doesn't know if she should leave or what. Try "Haven't I seen you at Dance Home?" It probably won't work, but hey.

7. Iconic Papier-Mâché Folk Art; Skeletons or Animals:

This woman is a former art student who is currently into designing her own jewelry and clothing. She is probably starving. Definitely get her card—it will be unlike any business card you have ever seen. She lives with her boyfriend, also from CalArts, who makes microtonal instruments out of discarded steel pipes and dourly rages at the Independent Composers Association for refusing to fund a retrospective. Now he's considering film scoring. Neither actually has a job. They are a neat art couple living in one of those funky decaying Echo Park houses that seems to be gradually sliding down the hillside into the lake. "I've just been admiring your fabulous earrings!" is an excellent start, of course, since she made them.

8. Large Silver Buttons, Gold Leaves, etc.:

When a woman really wants to meet a man *tonight,* she is not going to take chances on inordinately clever accessories that may or may not work. She wants things that catch light from fifteen feet away and make her look like a fox. Probably the hair will be beautifully loose. A skintight black dress. Black hose. Killer heels. The thing to do is to swing by, look into her eyes, and say, enunciating clearly: "Sexy dress." Then immediately disappear into the crowd. Hide in the bathroom, in the broom closet, wherever. She'll be tossing her hair back often and using those moments to quickly scan the room for you over the shoulders of the countless hesitant men who talk to her nervously about film. Wait patiently.

9. Asymmetrical or Mismatched Earrings:

Either this woman has made a tragic mistake she doesn't know about, or this is her fashion statement. If it is the latter, she really is interested only in meeting someone European.

10. Postmodern Icons:

a) 24-K Resistors:

She got these earrings at the LACE bookstore and frankly, she's not entirely sure they work. She loved the tongue-in-cheek reference to technology, but nobody so far has commented. Perhaps they've never seen an electrical circuit before, so they don't even know what these things are! Anyway, she just graduated from USC, is now doing some copyediting at *High Performance* magazine, will look into doing some interning at KPFK. Would like perhaps to be an art critic, not sure. "I don't know. You look really familiar to me—do you dance with Mary Jane Eisenberg?" will make her putty in your in hands.

b) Miniature Gold Picture Frames Containing Autographed Photos of the Bloated Elvis:

Black sweater, riding pants, buzz haircut, smoking. Okay, okay. She has had some success with her post-feminist multimedia performance show and she doesn't care who knows it. Thinking of taking it to New York, maybe Berlin. Some guy from HBO approached her about video possibilities. What is this magazine *Critique of America* she saw in a restaurant the other day—should she be profiled in it or what? "I am the editor of *Interview* magazine and I have been combing the continent for you for ten years" should break the ice pretty well.

A Survey
of Open-Mike
Poetry Readings

First it was Harley Davidsons, it seems, and now this: When even Justine Bateman is glimpsed casually essaying a few lines of self-penned poesy at Cafe Largo (where, coincidentally, "you're not allowed to read unless you're a celebrity," according to one disgruntled performance-poet), it becomes clear that "spoken word" has hit this city in a big way. Poetry's current vogue, however, has relatively little to do with the fact that even Los Angeles people who aren't famous—perhaps partially because they are Los Angeles people who aren't famous—have always loved poetry, particularly their own. Open-mike poetry readings dot our fair city like a slew of unusual and sometimes somewhat bedraggled flowers, to a point where "the church of the open mike" is happening somewhere in the city every night of the week.

Best Open Mike
for the Shy

The Espresso Bar attracts 1) orators, 2) monologists, 3) bards, 4) sages, 5) soothsayers, 6) ordinary folks, 7) Ted Soqui. Wednesday nights here tend to shamble along at an unhurried pace. Amiable host Don Kirby starts things off at about 9:55 P.M., and by 10:07 everyone who wanted to has read a poem. "Surely there must be somebody out there who wants to read," Kirby offers. "Notes scribbled on napkins, anything?" No response—by now the espresso machine is whirring and half the room is shouting at each other in conversation. After tossing out a few tentative riffs of his own ("Time flies when you're alive" "It's never too late to say yes"), Kirby reads a few lines from the works of Gary Snyder. He trails off. A bystander takes up the mike and talks a little about his day. Eventually, a shy, middle-aged man creeps forward. None too close to the mike, he begins reading in a quavering voice from a dog-eared book of poetry. Over the roar of the room, one line suddenly gels, rubylike in its mystery: "I feel the explosion of each pleasure cell."

Best Open Mike
for the *Really, Really* Shy

Who was that extraordinarily serious blonde girl who was writing pages and pages of verse in her notebook, stopping every now and then to sigh, and never got up to read? Certainly she was a shy person who cannot share a love poem or two ("I can no longer keep these feelings inside!") at Lizards, perhaps one of the most subdued and polite of open readings. Etiquette tips from Emily Post are even read out loud here.

Best Open Mike
for the Five-Minute Novellini

Let's just say that your average urban-dwelling gay poet can do more in five minutes than many accomplish in an hour. Take Fred Anderson, for instance, whose self-described "three poems and a novellini" sported pithy openings like this: "Because I could not stop for him/he kindly stopped for me in a brown Triumph with the top down." ("Homage or pillage of Emily Dickinson?" John Rechy might ask.) Now it is true that visiting college student Frederick Bertz, unusually wide-eyed for the savvy crew packing A Different Light, saw gay experiences in terms of rhyming couplets, actually attempting to use "closet" as a poetic meta-phor. And we know that this demonstrates that even the com-plexly sensual, often potently ironic world of gay poetry will have its Suzanne Somerses. But unlike Bertz, Ms. Somers never had to deal with being reviled as the campus "rag queen," as far as we can tell from her autobiography. In other words, Bertz's work still had resonance. Altogether, the mood at A Different Light's an-nual reading is warm, empathetic, and celebratory of a number of voices. As MC James Pickett quipped to Bertz, "You just keep wearing those skirts, honey, and ignore those dried-up old hip-pies at Santa Cruz."

Best Open Mike
for Ocean-Going Thetans

After dodging squads of radiant Scientologists—resplendent in their handsome Navy SEA ORG uniforms—bustling along the halls of the ornate Celebrity Centre International, one reaches Poetry by Candlelight. Held in the plush La Renaissance Restaurant, the emphasis here is on *splurging*. Poetry by Candlelight is perhaps the only open-poetry reading in town where someone could read a ten-minute-long poetic history of the universe called "Buddha in My Heart" (preceded by a fifteen-minute autobiographical introduction studded with layman's explanations of key terms like "thetan" and "buddhi"), ask that fateful two-word question ("One more?"), and receive a chorus of eager "Yes!'s." Unlike in your average limit-obsessed reading, there is no time limit here and there are no ominous questions like "How many more pages, Randall?" which tend to interrupt the spontaneous flow.

Best Open Mike
for Those Who Welcome
an Alternative to
Spending a Rough Night
Curled Up on
Hollywood Boulevard

Arts dollars may come and go, but Hollywood Underground co-ordinator Howard Finkelstein deserves praise for his commitment—and courage—in single-handedly producing a year-round "Open Festival" during the graveyard hours smack in the festering maw of Hollywood. Indeed, the new Gorky's is itself kind of an anomaly in its Cahuenga site, located as it is only blocks from Ziganne Fashion string bikinis (where each C-cup seems to be held up by its own precarious pulley system), several fine Hollywood Boulevard wig shops, and, of course, the ever-frightening Tomy's No. 5.

The Hollywood Underground, however, is relatively free of that off-kilter, glittery-eyed, Hollywood street energy that tends to make the hysterical letters "PCP! PCP!" flash on and off in the middle-class brain as one tries to act very casual. On our visit, the Underground functioned as a safe harbor for unlikely bedfellows: comics a little unsteady on their feet, emerging songwriters, some folks who just seemed glad to have a clean, well-lit place to sit at three in the morning. Overall, the group united in a positive, Midnight Mission way: a sing-along of some calypso tune about Jamaica and rum led by an elderly man in suspenders at the piano got a pretty good response. Indeed, one could sit there with a mug of warm milk and ponder the shaky progress of *anyone's* career, the theme of homelessness feeling like not such a bad metaphor at Gorky's at three A.M.

Best Open Mike for the Unsightly Blab

"I keep your sperm out of toilets."
—Tequila Mockingbird
performance-poetess and
Zatar's bartender

Some called it "A Bad Night at the Blab"; some called it "Open Mike at Zatar's"; others called it, simply, "A Nightmare on Wilcox Avenue." There is something unutterably dark about a full-grown woman talking vociferously about her CLIT to a murky barful of strangers who look like escapees from the set of *Blade Runner.* There is something about being told, through caustically narrowed eyes, "I see you squeeze out your little hard turds of love." (Although doesn't that line somehow ring true? Oh, well.) There is something about a man in a skull shirt reading a fifteen-page monologue about gunning young Asian girls to pieces. In short, it was the kind of evening in which an open mike becomes more like an open hole.

Poetic MC and bon vivant Mike "High on the Spoken Word" Mollett was honestly bewildered by what Club Blab has unleashed. As he confided later, the Blab was originally conceived as a lively, off-the-book, spontaneous rap between a performer and an audience, i.e., "blab." Not that standard readings are bad, but Mollett finds them rather stationary. In his own words: "The word bursts from the mouth, throbbing, shattering the airwaves!

The word is a virus infesting cities!" He meant that in a nice way. Mollett would like those interested to know that partner-in-blab Doug Knott is back from his tour and there are themes now—sex, car troubles, drugs, TV, to name a few—so the magic of Blab has apparently returned.

The Writer Within

Let me tell you, Los Angeles is hell on writers. I'm referring to unpublished, unproduced writers with no connections and maybe not the greatest sense of plot structure either. I expect the rest do rather well.

I'm referring, of course, to me—and my unfinished Novel. My Novel, thank you for asking, is about Los Angeles in the 1990s. Not the clichéd glitzy Los Angeles, but the Los Angeles no one knows. Unfortunately, not even *I* know it very well, which is why the whole thing seems to have keeled over on page ninety-three. One of my characters found himself raising a glass of Chablis at a quiet little dinner party in Glendale, opening his mouth, and . . .

"God, this is dull!" he cried out suddenly, collapsing onto a rather unusual tartan love seat I'd spent the previous three pages describing. There he sits to this day, smoking and irritable.

At least I had the good sense to give up on the Screenplay. Screenplays do have some advantages over novels: they're only 120 pages, mostly white space, and can make you a lot of money.

But what do you do with them when you're done? No one in my crowd knows anybody in the Industry. We pretend to: "Did you hear that Sue is reading for Paramount?" someone will throw out impressively, smearing faintly oldish pâté onto a stale cracker. But these connections always evaporate.

Screenplay "pitching" is difficult, too, as I learned in that carnival-of-abuse known as the adult-ed screenwriting course. Offered by the USC School of Continuing Education, it had a hideous title—"The Business of Screenwriting"—and met at night in a classroom with little student desks. It seemed as far from God and Hollywood as one could imagine. Fluorescent lighting bathed our slump-shouldered squad in a kind of zombie hue.

Joe, an ailing, grizzled fellow in his fifties (think Raymond Burr sans health insurance), was toting a seven-hundred-page script "about child molestation and the Vietnam War." Eager-eyed Robert was a parking attendant at Universal Studios: this was his Industry "connection." "I can get you all in," he promised, casual. Liz had Coke-bottle glasses and hair like a fright wig. When asked her interests, she piped out one happy word: "Elves!"

No wonder our teacher, who shall remain nameless (Ken Stevens), loathed us. But he loathed us so deeply we weren't even aware of it; we thought he *liked* us. So it goes, I guess, with therapists-turned-agents. Nor was he a big agent. His major "credit" was that he had once been the partner of a guy who had briefly "handled" James Brolin.

Witness how we begin the gradual slide down the Industry food chain: Every week Ken Stevens would bring in a new "professional colleague" to hear us pitch. Such colleagues were mostly short, stocky, mean-spirited men sporting too-small leather jackets, male-pattern baldness, and Jovan Musk for Men.

The one I remember most vividly was producer Sandy Leibman, who had one or two movies in the bikini/slasher/kickboxing genre to his credit. There I was, nervously practicing my pitch for a TV series "concept" (in case Aaron Spelling were to phone). At that time, *Hotel,* with Connie Sellecca, was big; my idea was to do a show called *Motel*—the weekly travails of maybe not-so-glamorous but perhaps more human people who worked the front desk at Motel 6. . . .

My voice gradually trailed off into silence.

"Is this supposed to be a comedy?" Sandy Leibman asked.

"Uh—maybe. Perhaps."

Sandy shoved his face into mine, teamster style. "THEN WHY AM I NOT LAUGHING?"

What it boiled down to was that I was a person completely without "concept." Screenplay writing is this lean, clean, aerobicized form full of "plot points" that wheel about suddenly (He murders her!) and poke one in the eye like an angry silicone breast. The screenplay is a thong bikini, exposing all structural flaws. I and my pear-shaped musings were advised to cover ourselves in the loose old bathrobe of the novel.

Despairing, I crossed town and flung myself into the waters of UCLA Extension. But how balmy they were! Tears of surprised joy came to my eyes. "I am home," I whispered, thumbing through the catalog, "I am home." This was how I had dreamed writing could be—classes along the lines of "Writing Children's

Books in One Day," "Dancing Your Own Autobiography," "Finding the Writer Inside and Giving Her a Massage," "Doing Haiku to Find Your Scream."

Creativity without threats, in short. And I'm for it. You know how some people (a.k.a. hearty Jeff in accounting) hand over their manuscript and declare, "Be brutally honest"? Not me. My ego is fragile. What I want to say when I hand you my Novel is: "Imagine this is the autobiography your eighty-year-old aunt with the weak heart and two weeks to live has been writing for the past thirty years; you figure largely in her will; don't upset her."

I finally chose a class that seemed to be a happy medium between the slasher and haiku schools, a course entitled "Writing the Novel the Professional Way." If not, "Finishing the Novel the Professional Way." Who says we should all finish a book in ten weeks? American Book Award–winner Harriet Doerr published her first book, *Stones for Ibarra,* at seventy-three. (*"Stones for Ibarra! Stones for Ibarra!"* is a good mantra, I've found, for struggling, would-be novelists to chant.)

But completion—or at least closure—was a lesson many of us needed. The manuscripts fellow students were dragging around were practically moldering. Massage therapist Jenny, after seven years of "making notes" on her historical romance, had yet to finish a first draft. Don, in insurance, discussed his college memoir, *Don and Carol,* at every break. "I've been working on it since 1976!" he enthused. "I've taken this class five times!"

More memorable, though, was Marguerite, a lovely, faintly sad-looking fortyish educator—blonde hair streaked lightly with silver, cashmere sweater, beige scarf. She described her novel with simple dignity: "A forty-seven-year-old woman married unhappily for twenty-three years spends the summer alone in rainy England, where she has time to think over all the regrets of her life. . . ."

Maybe our novels are things we don't *want* to finish, I thought. Like cloaks, we hold them against us to protect ourselves from that harsh, cold world out there. Once we let go, they often just fall to the ground to be trampled . . . by Sandy Leibman wearing Jovan Musk for Men.

It

Happened

in Glendale

Do I believe in the magic of Disney? Why yes, I do.

One day my friend Roger Cox was a forty-something under-employed actor/director/pet-sitter. The next, he blossomed into a veritable Industry mini-mogul, sporting capped teeth, brand-new Isuzu Trooper, and even health insurance.

Sound miraculous, Cinderella-esque, late-eighties? It is. And it could have happened only in Glendale—at the Walt Disney Corporation.

The story begins in a little ramshackle bungalow, sans air-conditioning, in Pasadena. The year is 1985. Our hero has just stepped off the plane from New York, penniless, with only a duffle bag.

L.A. is a place where appearances mean a lot. And let us just say that in fall 1985, Roger does not look like a person who will soon be playing tennis in Encino. He is forty-one going on seventy, a battered five foot three ("a root-beer dwarf" is his self-description), a chain-smoker, a lousy dresser, and has bad knees.

Equity-waiver theater can be a cruel mistress, and after thirty-five she can inflict a certain darkness of spirit. ("She takes all your money and after a while won't even fuck you anymore," as my friend Mel says.) Because thirty-five is an age when even the most die-hard Bohemian begins to wish for life's little luxuries: one's own futon to sleep on, liability car insurance, dental care.

Roger has none of these things. So add to the appearance a somewhat negative life outlook. But this is all soon to change. *How* is almost Hans Christian Andersen-esque.

Fast forward to 1987. Roger is tapped to direct an original play in a not untypical seventy-seven-seat L.A. run—six weeks of rehearsal culminating in one weekend of performance. Meanwhile, someone loses six thousand dollars, there are no reviews, and frantic efforts to videotape it at some tiny college in Pomona with hostile student cameramen come to nothing.

The final insult: Monday morning, Roger, *the director*, is forced to drive all the props and furniture back himself.

Picture it. There our hero sits on a blazing Monday morning—and how cruel those L.A. Monday mornings are—at a stoplight (Western and Santa Monica) in his uninsured '79 Honda Civic.

But then, something makes Roger look to his left. And there, gesturing at him madly, is a well-groomed woman in a cream-colored Audi.

"Roger Cox!" she calls out. He rolls down his window. "John is in town! He wants you to call him!" A phone number is hurled into the shuddering Honda, followed by the screech of Audi tires.

One week later, boom! Roger is hired by Disney. And why not? Disney's amusement park division is expanding, expanding, expanding. They're building up Disneyworld in Orlando like crazy, next is Euro Disney, and then there's Japan! They need creative . . . thinkers!

Roger is suddenly drawing sixty thousand dollars a year—perhaps four times what he's ever seen in his forty-odd years. Job description? "Imagineer." Now, many of us have brilliant, idiosyncratic, cantankerous friends who we think do not quite fit into this world—and certainly not into this thing called Entertainment Industry. They chain-smoke their way into angry girlfriends' homes in Reseda, reading Tolstoy while everyone else goes off to their day jobs.

Who ever hears of them suddenly striking gold? Who even knew that there was even a job called an "Imagineer"?

"Roger . . . thinks up rides for amusement parks," I would tell other Bohos, semi-employed thirty-somethings active in their various part-time songwriting/freelance recording engineer/jewelry design/eight-dollar-an-hour word processing/unpublished novelist/studio bass trombone/pot-selling industries. "Wow," such creative types respond, their eyes glazing over.

And, at the end of the evening, Roger would unfailingly pick up the check. His triumphal cry: "It's on the Mouse!"

Roger came to have a dapper new look, too. Once on the Disney lot—where you meet a better class of people anyway—he had almost immediately met a fine new woman who made it her mission to get the Tweeds catalog and buy Roger everything out of it. Soon Roger is resplendent in safari khakis and beige linens and crisp white shirts.

He trades in the Civic for a Trooper. The hair is permed, teeth are capped, new glasses are purchased. Roger begins to look positively sleek. In his equity-waiver days, he used to call Industry scouts, with great derision, "the IJS"—which stood for "Important Jewish Suits." Now he is one. He quits smoking. He pays off some twenty-odd years of debt.

Roger begins to hire his poorer artistic friends for Walt Disney Imagineering (WDI) gigs. He is Solomon dispensing coins to the peasants: voice-overs flow from him, a music score for a three-minute in-house film, hundred-dollar checks for two hours of concept-consulting.

Roger is absolutely in his element. Never was a job so suited to a person. Calls roar in from him Monday morning. "Asia!" he exclaims in stentorian tones. "What do you find fascinating about Asia? Go!" Apparently, this week's task is to think up rides based on the continents. But why stop there? Next week, his assignment is: "The Universe!"

But then, the tide turns.

Was it an angry look from Michael Eisner? One bloated Visa bill too many? A bad dream about a Mouse?

"Agenbite of inwit," is Roger's three-word explanation. And when a Disney person begins quoting Joyce, that is the point where you know you will soon be paying for your own drinks. Roger begins staying in over the weekend, reading Nietzsche, Boll, books about the Grand Guignol Theater.

Ask him how "Asia!" and his close friend Jeffrey Katzenberg are doing, and one gets only a curt response: "I'm tired of writing for robots!"

In the next breath, Roger goes into wild tirade. Excitedly he outlines his new project: to perform *Krapp's Last Tape* in the Theatre/Theater toilet, pants down around his ankles, for three people.

He is smoking again.

You know he's finally gone over the edge when he tells you he is thinking of designing a new amusement park concept called "Shit Land." Here terrible shit happens to people, and uniformed "Shit Landers" cheerfully abuse them. . . .

Fortunately for Roger, the world economy turns. And soon the amusement park industry is to go into a little bit of a bust. In short, in summer 1992, the unthinkable happens: Disney lays off some four hundred of its five hundred Imagineers. (Even though, oddly, the construction of new buildings and wings continues apace.)

The nightmare is over. Roger is free again. And he is at peace.

After all, he's had five great years, thanks to his corporate fairy godmother. His debts are paid off. He's got a terrific wardrobe. He has money in the bank. He's got contacts (both in his address book and in his eyes). He can collect unemployment now, do nothing but dream for a year.

For a guy who came here with nothing, that's pretty good.

Next stop? It's certainly not New York.

But Roger does have an application in to teach university drama. And all I can say is, the state of Montana had better watch out.

Is This
Ethnic
Enough
for You?

In 1989, at the age of twenty-seven, I learned I was "Asian."

Of course, I had partly brought my sudden Asian-ness upon myself. In 1986, I had begun using my full (Chinese) name: I thought that while "Sandra Loh" sounded dull, "Sandra Tsing Loh" was a good name for a performance artist. It sounded experimental. It implied, "Anything can happen." Like Yoko Ono, I might suddenly spin around and marry a Beatle! You get the idea.

But no. In the late eighties and early nineties, having a name like Sandra Tsing Loh meant something else. It meant that I was "multicultural" and, as a result, the object of a lot of sudden interest. Producers of small arts festivals who had never before paid much attention to my work began phoning me up to see if I was working on anything related to my racial heritage. (In 1991, for instance, they were always looking to see if I had any performance pieces dealing with my response as a member of an ethnic minority to the Columbus quincentenary.)

I also began getting enthusiastic phone messages from former colleagues now clearly on the career track in the arts-administration world—messages like "I know you're not really into dance, but I've just been elected to the board of a commission to create a spring arts festival in the downtown area—and we need a Korean dance troupe. Do you know any? You can tell them we're paying real money on this one. We have a grant!"

Which brought me to another revelation.

While I, like an idiot, had been waging my own quasi-Byronic artistic war against the world at large, being dramatically broke all the time, never receiving a dime of grant money, there was a real, ongoing arts economy in Los Angeles that provided checks for artists. Which was actually quite good news. For despite the success of my piano performance "spectacles," which have been covered (for the most part approvingly) in the likes of *People* magazine, the *Wall Street Journal,* and the *Los Angeles Times,* as well as on CNN and even in Johnny Carson's monologue, and despite the estimated one thousand people who attended my most recent outdoor event—I was broke.

That's because since 1987 I have lost something on the order of $10,000—the price of two great used cars or an Alaskan cruise for four or one hundred pairs of (sale-priced) Bruno Magli shoes. Production costs for my productions have ranged from $1,400 (cheap) for a Harbor Freeway piano concert to $5,500 (stressful) for a single midnight show for spawning grunion, performed live on a Malibu beach by a thirty-five-piece orchestra.

So there I was, reading in the paper every other day about artists I knew who were getting $8,000 grants for one-person shows. The thought that I might not have to live in poverty in order to keep making art seemed astonishing.

As I was soon to find out, however, getting on the art dole of the nineties meant making a pact—if not with the devil, then at least with the czars of L.A.'s new multiculturalism, and those folks run as tight an arts "ship" as the Medicis.

I. The "New" Internationalism

At some point in the eighties, the word *multicultural* replaced the word *international*, and the rest wasn't history. At least not for art in Los Angeles.

International—what a guileless, friendly word. As a kid in the sixties, I remember drinking up everything international: Expo '67! UNICEF! The five intertwining rings of the Olympics! International . . . House of Pancakes! "Come in!" international people always seemed to be saying. "We don't care where the hell you're from. Have some flapjacks!"

For our family, food was indeed an ethnic clearinghouse, albeit a bland one. Being Chinese-German meant having rice *and* potatoes with every meal. It meant some days you'd study little Chinese flashcards and get lectured in algebra by Dad; others you'd be driven, with tires screeching, to ballet and piano lessons by Mom. In fact, much of the time being international meant having so many lessons you just wanted to keel over.

But in the end, it was all worth it. Because international people were always trying to smile and embrace and work together to achieve amazing things—competing in the pole vault, playing the violin like a virtuoso, ending world hunger.

Then, as internationalism waned in the self-centered seventies, a new aesthetic called multiculturalism washed up on the dreary beaches of academe. Unlike internationalism, which viewed the world through the rose-colored lens of global brotherhood, multiculturalism was concerned about making sure everyone got a piece of the pie. Unlike international people, multicultural people seemed to spend much of their time hurling things at each other and fighting over gristly little bits of grant money.

In the arts, multiculturalism has somehow become prized over all other qualities—over talent, over beauty, over ideas. As a result, emerging playwrights are suddenly rediscovering their one-sixteenth Cherokee roots. Second-generation Asian-American actresses who never even bothered to learn Chinese are suddenly yearning for their grandmothers in Shanghai (not enough to go there, perhaps, but enough to do a monologue about it). And Caucasians are suddenly developing pieces about the terrible angst of having no actual ethnic roots on which to base their art.

II. Multiculturalism: It's the Law!

In Los Angeles, the commissariat of artistic multiculturalism is a branch of city government known as the Cultural Affairs Department. In 1988, this department took control of the L.A. Endowment, a grants program for local arts supported by about twenty-five million dollars in municipal funds. With that, an era was launched.

Since a movement is nothing without a manifesto, the L.A. Endowment paid $294,999 to a consulting firm to draft one for them. The result, issued in November 1990, was the rather ominously named "Cultural Masterplan," a study that cites everything from the history of the National Endowment for the Arts to the problems Asians have with driving long distances.

Though the sheer bulk of the Masterplan's ten volumes puts Aristotle's unfinished *Poetics* to shame, a quarter of a million dollars initially seems a lot to pay for such stunning insights as "Both the Arts Advisory Committee and the Los Angeles Task Force on the Arts recognize the artist as the originator of art activity."

To be fair, the Masterplan does quickly pick up speed, its central thesis being: "Los Angeles should distinguish itself as an international art center through the development of its multicultural character." Art, the manifesto reveals, is three things: a cultural equalizer, therapy, and a catalyst for social change. The Masterplan then goes on to outline its mission—and display its politically correct mind-set—in bold, forbidding strokes. To wit:

The arts must reflect the multicultural nature and profile of Los Angeles . . .

One of the biggest problems in arts programming is that arts audiences are White . . .

It is necessary to address past inequities in order to establish and appreciate a cultural life truly reflective of the city's heterogeneous population . . .

Defining "quality" by Western European standards may not be acceptable to many cultural and ethnic groups . . .

As numerous racial, ethnic, and cultural groups assume their place in the public arena that constitutes Los Angeles' vitality, definitions of quality must be expanded and restated in new historical terms . . .

The allegations of lowering standards and decreasing quality are often specious smoke screens for cultural intransigence . . .

Consistent vigilance is necessary to assess whether established policies and processes are helping to achieve cultural equity and diversity.

III. Mendelssohn: A Fine Composer of Jewish Heritage

Vigilant indeed the Cultural Affairs Department has been. Soon after it began making grants, even well-established, politically correct nonprofit institutions were being felled by the big ax of diversity.

Shakespeare/LA and the Padua Hills Playwrights Festival, for example, were initially denied funds in 1991, despite a history of assembling multiracial casts, printing bi- and trilingual programs, presenting free shows in underprivileged areas, and even collecting cans of food for the needy. A lack of both community support and multiculturalism was cited as the reason. What about those ethnically diverse casts? According to the Cultural Affairs Department, they didn't count for anything without documentation. The free Shakespeare productions? Again, no dice—the company hadn't provided any lesson plans to make the material directly relevant to inner-city kids.

The lengths to which cultural institutions will go to placate the Cultural Affairs Department would be laughable—if they weren't often so desperate. Consider the case of the L.A. Solo Repertory Orchestra. In its 1990 grant application, it proposed putting on a concert that would feature a high-school student soloist selected by open audition. The publicity for the concert was to be distributed through the L.A. school district (thereby serving both education and the community—an impressively grant-worthy stratagem). In addition, as a response to the Eurocentric historical bias of those benighted souls who might mistakenly prefer to celebrate 1992's Columbus quincentenary, there was to be a concert featuring usually neglected non-Western composers.

For all that, when it reviewed the orchestra's grant proposal, the Cultural Affairs Department thought it detected some slight blurring of the group's motives—some deficiency in its commitment to true diversity. As a result, it rejected the application, noting: "Repretoire [*sic*] could include more works by Afro-American composers."

Not surprisingly, the orchestra appealed the rejection, summarizing its argument thus: "The applicant refutes the panel's comments regarding supporting Afro-American and other ethnic composers by stating it has performed most of [African-American composer] William Grant Stills's work, introduced a Japanese concerto into its '90-'91 season, and presented an Afro-American soloist, in addition to presenting Mendelssohn, who has a Jewish heritage."

One can only salute the touching bravery of the L.A. Solo Repertory Orchestra in its sinking, flaming ship, trying at the eleventh hour to slip Mendelssohn past the Guardians of Culture. And indeed, the panel was unimpressed by Mr. Mendelssohn's alleged Hebraic lineage. "[C]laiming that Mendelssohn is not Euorcentric [*sic*]," they noted, "is stretching it."

IV. "And Now I'd Like to Salute That Beloved Chinese Philosopher Charlie Chan."

In a more positive vein, perhaps we should look at what multiculturalism is ideally supposed to be.

News Item No. 1 (*Los Angeles Times,* July 28, 1991): Twenty-eight-year-old inner-city artist Sandra Drinning receives $8,000 to paint a 16 x 94–foot mural depicting the whole of Los Angeles, funding to come from the Social and Public Art Resource Center (SPARC), nearly 60 percent of whose $700,000 annual budget is provided by the Cultural Affairs Department via the L.A. Endowment. Says SPARC spokesman Eric Gordon: "It is by far the most detailed mural in the city. But perhaps more importantly, it is the most ethnically unifying mural in the city."

Explains artist Drinning: "I wanted to depict every type of person, from the homeless to the privileged. And through architecture, I wanted to depict different ethnic groups. Watts Towers represents blacks; Mann's Chinese [Theater], Asians; Olvera Street, Latinos; Beverly Hills, whites; and, of course, this supermarket represents the Korean community."

OK, I know: even the greatest artists make generalizations they'd be hard-pressed to justify under sufficiently demanding circumstances—say, on a bus ride through downtown. But given our heightened ethnic sensitivities these days, Drinning's mural strikes me as being doubly disingenuous. For one thing, it reinforces negative stereotypes of minorities. I mean, is her next mural going to be a full-on portrait of that great Chinese philosopher Charlie Chan? And for another, it glosses over a few inconvenient details—such as the fact that the Watts Towers were actually constructed by an Italian-American, that the Chinese Theater was built by Hollywood Jews, and that what we now call Beverly Hills was first settled by Hispanics.

V. The Rise of Art Gangs

The new tribalism that characterizes today's art scene began amid much enthusiasm—an enthusiasm originally stoked by mere competition for attention. I think back to one of the early Open Festival meetings at Barnsdall Park in 1989. The Open Festival consisted of uncurated, unfunded, non-theme-oriented artists—in short, your basic arts chattel. (I count myself, with my *Music for the Bonus Carwash* piece, among this multitude.) Excitement at this meeting ran high, for L.A. Festival director Peter Sellars, the internationally renowned theatrical *wunderkind* and winner of one of those MacArthur Foundation "genius" grants, was actually coming down from on high to speak with us. He cared!

Sellars began his oration by presenting us with a sweeping vision of an L.A. Festival in which 75 percent of the events would be free and outdoors, and in which what had been "fringe" would now occupy "the center." What he was proposing was no less than a twenty-first-century revolution in the performing arts.

Having thus raised his banner, he took questions.

And what questions we had! Open Festival participants kept leaping to their feet, asking things like "And what about the Serbo-Croatian community? Will there be arts representation there?" Or "For the last few months, our group has been doing performances for elderly shut-ins. What is the commitment of the festival to this?" (Applause.) At one point, a rotund little fiftyish woman leapt up and declared portentously, "*Yiddishkeit* is coming!" (*Yiddishkeit* was the name of her one-woman show.)

This unmelting of the melting pot got worse when the formal grant season began. Groups of minority artists who once spoke of a great "rainbow" coalition now found themselves up against a hard economic fact: there was only so much money to go around. As a result, "art gangs" began forming up. Today, these gangs roam the city, recruiting the right people with the right backgrounds, weeding out the heretics who fail to conform to Masterplan specifications. This is not to say that there are actual drive-by shootings involving competing folk-dance troupes—although who's to say what might happen if the funding crunch grows worse?

But cultural separatism is in full flower; it's even financially rewarded! Consider the following grant awards culled from a recent issue of the *Cultural Affairs Department Bulletin*: $5,000 to the Zoryan Institute (Armenian folk arts), $3,000 to the World Kulintang Institute (Philippines), $10,000 to the United Latinos for the Arts, $4,951 to the Southern California Indian Center, $5,000 to the Streisand Center for Jewish Cultural Arts, $1,000 to the Korean Artist Association of Southern California, $1,000 to the IGBO Cultural Association (Nigeria), $2,500 to An Claidheamh Solius (Celtic dance and music), $2,500 to the American Croatian Club, and on and on.

Indeed, cultural separatism was the explicit theme of an odd little incident that occurred last year in conjunction with a group known as the Queens Historical Society. The society had received $5,000 from the L.A. Endowment to produce an event called Evening on the Nile, part of which (*Queens of the Nile, Now!*) was described as an ancient Egyptian fashion show. That this program was presented as part of the Fifth Annual World Melanin Conference, a black nationalist event, didn't seem to bother anyone. But things did get a little dicey when a representative of the Cultural Affairs Department was asked to leave the event because she was white—though not dicey enough for the L.A. Endowment to stop payment on its check.

In general, the Cultural Affairs Department seems to exhibit a marvelous tolerance for ethnocentrism—to the point of hiring members of the separatist Nation of Islam to provide security for its annual African Marketplace event.

One can only wonder what Mendelssohn would have thought of that.

VI. Extra! Extra!
Hot Arts
Grant Tip
of the Nineties!

One positive thing multiculturalism seems to have spawned is a healthy new candor about how minorities really feel about the majority. As a Cultural Affairs Department official put it in a recent newspaper interview: "Don't even bother applying if you're white."

VII. Spelling Is a Eurocentric
Skill, or Give a Man a Fish
and He Has But a Fish,
but Give a Man a Fishing Pole—
and He'll Make a Conceptual
Art Piece Out of It.

News Item No. 2 (*Los Angeles Times*, September 12, 1990): Coverage of the L.A. Festival includes a photo of a mural by an emerging minority artist who received $2,400 from the Cultural Affairs Department to do a series of collages made out of trash for a homeless center (actual cost of supplies: less than $150). The mural consists solely of the words "Abandonded [*sic*] Mind" painted on a wall. The artist is quoted as explaining the point of her mural thus: "Like abandoned mines, in which gold can sometimes be found, many of our people have underdeveloped resources when everyone else thought there was nothing there."

In the Masterplan's multicultural world, the "expanded" definition of quality apparently permits ethnically diverse people to make the leap directly to conceptual art without having to master simpler skills . . . like spelling. (Not that the offending artist had been educationally deprived: as it turned out, she had both an undergraduate degree and an M.A. in the humanities from Cal State Dominguez Hills.)

Then there are those popular programs for the truly disenfranchised, programs that actually involve the poor and the homeless in art. To be sure, such projects are well intentioned, enlightened, and even—on occasion—well reviewed (as was the L.A. Poverty Department's entry in the 1990 L.A. Festival). Still, in a nation reeling from a recession bordering on depression and a local economy with 8.5 percent unemployment, one wonders whether encouraging the homeless to put on plays is the most prudent use of public monies. I mean, is acting really a sensible career choice for a homeless person? Wouldn't putting money toward a decent apartment and a course in word processing do more good in the long run?

Not that many homeless people wouldn't make perfectly fine actors—but isn't the Screen Actors Guild the union with 95 percent unemployment?

VIII. And Now:
The Mel and
Sandra Show

So enough background—let's get to the foreground. Last fall, I was sitting around with my friend Mel Green (Irish-Hawaiian—or as he likes to say, "Top of the morning . . . Aloha"), planning a double bill of solo performances for Theatre/Theater, an eclectic performance space just off Hollywood Boulevard that doesn't use public money. As happens increasingly often these days, we began bemoaning the fact that although we've both paid our dues on the local solo performance circuit, we continually get passed over by all the new performance festivals—most of which now seem to have multiculturalism as their theme.

It's our own fault, I suppose. Though we're definitely not "mainstream" (you won't see us doing *Comic Strip Live* anytime soon), the fact is that Mel and I are fairly assimilated—meaning our ethnic background isn't our main concern. Also, we do not neatly fall into any of the "special constituencies" that the czars of artistic multiculturalism have deemed to be deserving of exceptional consideration.

As listed on the Cultural Affairs Grant Application, these worthy groups include abused children, AIDS patients, the disabled, drug users (well, we could try), gays, the homeless, and young people. To make matters worse, even though we don't do traditional theater, what we *do* do is not exactly in vogue right now.

I mean, hey, it's not that we turn down NEA grants. It's that we don't even get them in the first place! (Ironically, while I was researching and writing this story I did receive one grant—$480—for participating in a multiethnic performance at the Taper, Too.)

So there we were, brooding about all our disadvantages. And then we thought: How about throwing our own theater festival? We each knew several solo performance artists besides ourselves who, though talented and nonmainstream, also didn't score very high on the P.C. scale. Why not celebrate the work of this "unde-served" group?

We could call our event: Mel and Sandra's First Annual Mono-cultural Heterosexual Theater Festival!

We thought this was quite funny. But then we thought of some-thing funnier: How about satirizing the very notion of theater fes-tivals? Remember Martin Mull's *History of the White People in America*? Though apparently a parody of all those ethnic-awareness specials, Mull's real target, of course, was middle-class white people themselves, or at least the fact that most of what passed for their traditions were pretty boring (white bread and Jell-O leading my personal list).

So with that spirit in mind, we changed the title of our event to Mel and Sandra's First Annual Caucasian Heterosexual Theater Festival. We even roughed out some text for the accompanying program: "Performance artists Mel Green, Sandra Tsing Loh, et al. examine the experiences and consequences of being Cau-casian and heterosexual in America." And at the bottom: "This festival is supported in part by Mel's and Sandra's day jobs."

Mel and I figured we were the perfect people to put on an event like this. Since we're actually not white ourselves, how could anyone take offense?

We pitched the idea to Jeff Murray and Nicolette Chaffey, who run Theatre/Theater and have always demonstrated a taste for the absurd. Finding some humor in our idea, they promptly booked us in for two months' of Sundays. We then began signing up performers we knew, none of whom seemed to have a problem with what we thought was an obviously satiric title.

Early on in the signing-up process, I had a revealing conversation with a performer whose name I promised not to divulge. Let us just say that he was a Caucasian heterosexual whose work I greatly admire.

This, roughly, is an account of what transpired:

HIM: Caucasian Heterosexual Theater Festival? This isn't funny. This is offensive. I wouldn't want to be a part of this. This is hostile and racist.

ME: But how is this more hostile and racist than a gay Latino theater festival?

HIM: It sounds like you're encouraging gay bashing!

ME: But that's not our intention. We mean this in gentle humor. We're not attacking any particular group. If anything, we're satirizing performance art. Maybe if I sent you a mock-up of the flier—oh, forget it. What if I dropped the "heterosexual" part?

HIM: But *Caucasian*! I think you run the risk of attracting bad elements. It sounds like some white supremacist thing.

ME: When you can't call yourself Caucasian without implying you support Auschwitz, it's pretty sad. I think this is a new kind of racism.

Mel and I did our solo performance series last winter, renamed and recast as *A Freeway Home Companion.* We had evenings satirically entitled *Arts of the Atlantic Rim, The Emerging Caucasian Heterosexual Male Performance Workshop,* and the *Not Ready for PBS Players Present a Vaguely Multicultural Underfunded Event.* In the process, we presented black, Asian, female, Jewish, and gay performers—not because of their backgrounds, but because they happened to be excellent. Our audiences were large and enthusiastic.

Not a Nazi among them.

IX. Peter Sellars

If ever there was an example of a successful artist in the multicultural mode, Peter Sellars wouldn't be it.

Yes, he is multiculturalism's most eloquent spokesperson, the great verbal architect of Pacific Rim culture, a.k.a. L.A.'s new, non-Eurocentric vision of art. Still, I find it hard to believe that Pacific Rim art really works for him personally when he drops bombshells like "There will be no European works at all in the 1990 L.A. Festival!"—and then promptly flies off to New York to direct yet another production of *Cosi Fan Tutte.*

Then again, who can blame him? Would you turn down the chance to travel to rims Atlantic, Baltic, and Adriatic if someone else was paying for the tickets? Especially if you were allowed to use all those wonderful Western theatrical innovations—stuff like lights, sound systems, and the proscenium arch—without being criticized as Eurocentric?

What performer—even a multicultural one—really prefers to flail away giving free performances on a grassy plain while children and dogs mill about? To hell with the Pacific Rim and its populist requirements! I for one would rather have my pieces produced with the same advantages Peter Sellars enjoys: the Dorothy Chandler Pavillion, the Hollywood Bowl, and the L.A. Philharmonic, and high ticket prices.

Where will it all end? Many of us local artists who didn't fit into 1990's Pacific Rim theme now realize we won't fit into the next L.A. Festival either. Because the theme of that event is the Middle East. And remember, what counts is not just ethnicity, what counts is the specific tone of the work. Just as the fact that I happen to be Asian-American doesn't necessarily make my work Asian-American (at least in the eyes of the Guardians of Culture), artists of impeccably Middle Eastern descent may nonetheless find themselves excluded from the 1993 festival.

Will the theme of the L.A. Festival ever get around to "people who live in Los Angeles"? By the time it does, some of us are going to be selling real estate, in Seattle, probably.

Perhaps the theme of the festival should be money—cold, hard cash. After all, that's what everything always seems to come down to. Four years ago, I became so obsessed with the crippling financial sacrifices art seemed to demand that I withdrew one thousand dollars in one-dollar bills from my checking account and simply had them hurled over me as I played the piano. (I called the piece *Self-Promotion*.) Some two hundred people stampeded—including my own father, who told Channel 9, "I put her through college—and for the first time, I'm seeing money back!" (He managed to grab four dollars.)

The image that resulted was strange and beautiful: a sunny day, a thousand one-dollar bills floating in the air above four hundred hands—and then the wind shifting, the hands waving in unison after the bills, as natural as a school of minnows, while I, "the artist," got trampled underneath. I thought it had the odd ring of truth.

In the end, what counts is that my work has amused and delighted me. It doesn't really matter whether you or anyone else likes it or hates it; since I funded it all myself, I don't have to answer to anyone but myself. I always thought that was what artists did: They earned money and then spent it on the pieces they wanted to do, exactly the way they wanted to do them. As the Masterplan itself puts it, "Art originates with the artist."

Sure, self-funding can be a drag (I still drive a '73 VW). But then again, if someone else is paying for your work, doesn't that make him your boss? Isn't the artist supposed to be a sort of maverick, a guerrilla fighter who hovers on the outskirts of society, independent of it, critiquing it?

X. Mantovani:
The Official
Post-Multicultural Icon

When the burdens of multiculturalism become too great, I visit my father, an "actual" Chinese person. He is currently married to a Chinese woman named Zhou Ping, a very recent immigrant who is just beginning to learn English.

Since his retirement, my father's life has become very busy. He sets his alarm for three A.M. to learn French, Italian, and Spanish off the Arts & Entertainment Channel. He catches Karl Haas's show, *Adventures in Music*, on KUSC at ten A.M. At noon, there'll be a big Chinese meal cooked by Zhou Ping. Afterward, she'll uncork a few mandarin ditties for everyone's entertainment.

In the afternoon, Zhou Ping loves to watch Disney videos to learn English (her pleased quote: "*Cinderella*! It's very nice!"). And he'll maybe relax in the living room, where plastic busts of Mozart and Beethoven mingle before Chinese watercolors, and German chocolates are hidden in an Egyptian mosaic box.

Often, I hear him singing loudly, in his happy if hideously bad Italian: "Vo . . . la-re! Whoaaa-whoa! Vo . . . la-re! Ho ho ho ho!" Meanwhile, huge etchings of Lohs past—in their padded jackets and grim buns—glower down, not even imagining what the New World has wrought.

Part Two

Life in Suburbia

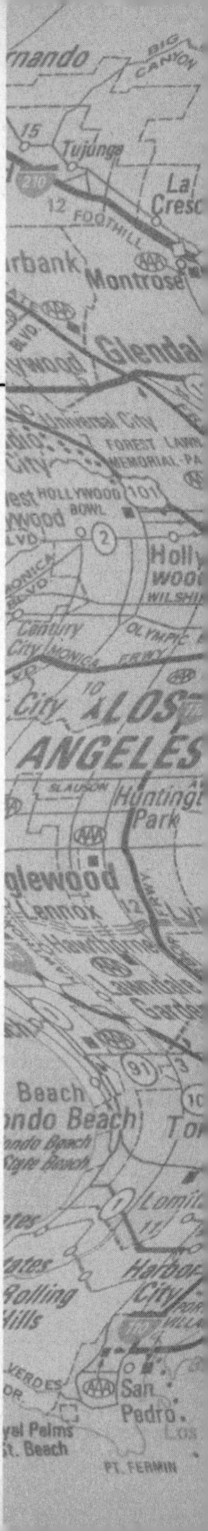

San Fernando
Sunland
Burbank
Hollywood
Studio City
West Hollywood
HOLLYWOOD BOWL
Century City
Culver City
Inglewood
Lennox
Redondo Beach State Beach
Rolling Hills
Royal Palms St. Beach

Joystick
Junkies

I'm a generous person. I'll give money, I'll give clothing, I'll give food. When my doorbell rings at five P.M., I answer it, cheerful and ready. Five dollars for a plutonium-hard candy bar to benefit a summer camp for runaway teenagers? Sure. My entire collection of circa 1991 Payless sandalwear for the poor? Of course. Six cans of Del Monte peas? No problem.

Just don't push me too far. . . .

It was a searing Valley afternoon. He came scraping up our driveway on his Big Wheel—five years old, Ninja Turtlewear cape. I heard the doorbell sound unevenly. I opened the hatch.

With nary a hello, he shoved a plastic cartridge upward. "Super . . . Mario?" he demanded.

All right. We obviously had Nintendo. Floating out over our yard was the telltale *ka-ching! ka-ching!* of dancing coins, mushrooms, and flowers; any canny neighborhood kid could hear it. My boyfriend, Mike, after his tough workday, had already been on it for a whole hour. Surely he wouldn't mind if little Martin (his name was scrawled on the cassette in a swift mother's hand) had a turn. . . .

Suddenly something inside me snapped. Involuntarily, my lips pulled back into a sneer and one shocking word came out: "No!"

And with it, I knew elation. It was the *no* I'd wanted to say one hundred times before. There I'd be at some dinner party, taking a much-needed break from the rigors of adult social interaction by amusing myself quietly in the corner with a Gameboy I'd found in the kitchen. I wouldn't be there two minutes before some seven-year-old would wrest it away. "Hey," he'd shrill. "Let me show you how to get to the waterfall land."

Children assume that Nintendo belongs to them and to them alone. Don't you dare grasp the joystick of a Sega Genesis demo system at Toys "Я" Us: "Can I do it?" asks a snub-nosed blond ten-year-old, elbowing his way in.

"Do you work?" would be my answer to that kid, little Martin, and to all children under twelve reading this column. (For all I know, the hordes may be looking up my address right now so they can climb my front gate with grubby game cartridges in hands.) "Do you pay taxes? I paid $110 for my Nintendo Entertainment System. What have you done?"

Sure I'm angry. Let the shorter humans play with what they've piled onto their own Visas. Being addicted to Nintendo and relishing the company of ten-year-olds are not synonymous.

Few remember that we children of the sixties—not Baby Boomers, but those of us who really *were* children in the sixties—had to grow up without Nintendo. As a child, I amused myself for hours with paper, pencil, and a few cracked wheels of Spirograph. I'd knit pot holders and stand wanly at the window, waiting for the bookmobile to arrive. High point of the week? *Kukla, Fran, and Ollie.* Plus we had those Von Trapp kids to think about, with their devilishly clever *Sound of Music* dance routines.

The curse of the sixties suburban childhood, of course, was that playtime was too intellectually challenging, too creative, too emotionally fulfilling. Struggle and reward. Struggle and reward. I peaked in fourth grade, reaching the unheard-of reading level of *turquoise* in SRA. For that achievement I got to be both Person of the Day and Nap Fairy. The other kids couldn't get up off their mats until I tapped them with my flower. I remember it as though it were yesterday.

It's no wonder I'm burned out today. I don't know what amusement is. I have zero hobbies, zero extracurricular interests. On the weekends, I don't throw clay, make dollhouses, do laundry, even. I'm burned out!

Adult life, I'm finding, is one long wait between meals. I don't know what's happening to my body, but I eat one potato chip and it flies right to my upper arms. I think about food all the time now that I can't have it. "Do I get to eat yet?" I ask myself every minute of the day. And when I finally do sit down at the table, it's "How much did I eat earlier? How much can I eat now?" (Do you remember the lunches—just lunches—we had in grade school? Bologna and American cheese on Wonder bread, squirt of mustard, Frito-Lay corn chips, Hostess Twinkies?)

Now it's only when I play Nintendo that I know bliss.

The perfect Saturday begins around two in the afternoon. A few palaces, a few goombas, and suddenly, refreshingly, it's time for the evening Pay-Per-View movie. In six hours I've eaten only a few handfuls of Trader Joe's barbecue chips and five Dannon low-fat pineapple yogurts. And half a muffin. And two Lite beers. So what? During that time I've also done an hour on the hated Combi Cycle 2000 stationary bike, which faces the Nintendo.

That's right—we Nintendo as we bike. See how productive? Struggle and reward. Struggle and reward. The good thing is, I'm now addicted to exercise. How many adults do you know who've done at least an hour of Nintendo five times a week for the past two years? My resting pulse-rate has gone up ten points, and I feel terrible. But look what I've accomplished: Super Mario 2; Super Mario 3; Dr. Mario (level 24, fast); Legend of Zelda; much of part 1 of Bart Simpson Versus the Space Mutants.

Check that out, you greedy munchkins! I certainly check you out via my monthly issue of *Nintendo Power Magazine.* (Why read *Newsweek?* Where is the pleasure?) How I hate you, you smug, bespectacled ten-year-olds (they run photos) who've completed Zelda Part II: The Adventures of Link and Battletoads. You say you like Dr. Mario and Krusty's Fun House, do you? Grrr. I have high scores and interesting opinions, too. Why am I not interviewed? Is it because I'm . . . thirty-one? This blatant ageism nauseates me.

My own Nintendo strengths are grim persistence and a cool, steely logic. I admit that I am a mercenary. I am not loyal to one cause. I go where I am called. I will save any princess in any castle. I will save any planet, crush any flying crab, no matter how rare a species. When I run into trouble, I just get more agile and more clever.

I'm less skilled when it comes to repeated punching and endless turbo speed-bike courses, which figure heavily in Battletoads.

So I vanquish those amphibians by extracting their game cartridge and hurling it against the wall. Next!

Or else I just break down and call the Game Tips Hotline. "This is a toll number," the voice says. "Please ask permission from your parents or whoever pays the phone bill." I do call my father, who says OK and wonders if I need a vacation. "With the lands I see on my Nintendo screen every day," I assure him, pitying his simplicity, "any other scenery would be a disappointment."

Party
Pooper

Conical polka-dot hats, squares of chocolate cake with confetti sprinkles on white icing, peppermint ice cream, gifts wrapped in Peanuts paper tucked slyly away in cupboards . . . who didn't used to love going to parties?

In kindergarten.

Oh, it was all so much fun then! Just receiving a Flintstones party invitation—or sending one out, being allowed to stick a ten-cent stamp on an envelope—was so thrilling I'd have to lie my head down on the Formica dining room table. What happened to all that energy, that sense of fun, that curiosity?

Today, I can't even pick up the telephone when it rings. That's how poorly I work and play with others. Talk about adulthood's diminished expectations. Picture me cringing over the answering machine—a kind of Nosferatu, Max Schreck–type figure in sweat-pants—as Monday's messages roll in. . . .

1. 7:23 A.M. My father (retired, lots of free time). Just what kind of car-insurance premium am I paying these days? Has just read an article in the *Los Angeles Times* that has him worried. Will clip and send. Please call back before eight (A.M.).

2. 9:17 A.M. Sharon Joss from *Southern California Consumer Trends* magazine, a division of SaveCo. Would like to assign a fifteen-hundred-word research piece on bookshelves! No pay, but pretty wide exposure—they have affiliates in Australia. She thinks.

3. 10:33 A.M. Hey! Louis again. When installing CareFree 3.6 for Windows, do you install the fonts separately in a whole other directory you create beforehand, or is that something you do on the second Options screen after initialization? Help!

4. 11:42 A.M. Women's-group meeting needs to be moved. Janet is leaving town weekend of twenty-first. Twenty-eighth is better, except Gail has to teach a class Saturday, making Friday the only good time, but of course traffic will be impossible for Jo, who is driving back from Pomona from her "Women and Prioritizing" conference. Open dates for meeting are now the twenty-fifth, twenty-seventh, or nineteenth of next month, but before twelve P.M. and after nine-thirty A.M. Please indicate availability.

You see? It's barely noon and I'm exhausted already. So when I hear message number five—inviting me to a party—I groan. Why would I want to go to a *party* on Saturday night? Why meet *new* people? I can barely handle the ones I already know. It hardly seems worth showering, poking earrings into lobes, and driving twenty-five minutes across town for . . . hey! That's another thing. In kindergarten, my mom always drove me to parties! On the way home I got to sleep off the cake and the Alvin and the Chipmunks sing-along in the backseat, my dress up around my head.

Compare that with what passes for fun these days. L.A. parties always seem to fall into three basic categories.

1. Parties held by and for people far more famous than you. Flashbulbs going off at the door are a pretty good indication you will be regarded as chattel inside. Beware of German or French male hairstylist/photographer assistant/blah-blahs. I know that nice members of this demographic exist, but let us say that a few bad apples have "accidentally" kicked shins in drink lines.

2. Parties held by and for your social peers. For me, this means everyone standing around rehashing their workweek while voraciously consuming room-temperature Trader Joe's products.

3. Parties held by people a few years and pieces of furniture behind you (i.e., the college dorm crowd). Expect to faithfully BYOB only to be greeted with a single bowl of Nacho Cheese Flavored Doritos under a bare light bulb, people in bicycle pants screaming and sweating around them. I have seen Lipton Onion Soup sour cream dip served, too. And battered M&Ms.

With this party, though, I couldn't gauge the category. The message gave only an address and time; the party host, a nice enough guy, I knew only vaguely. Anyway, perhaps I overcategorize, judge things too readily before experiencing them. Where was my sense of adventure? This was Saturday night, dammit!

Perhaps I'd meet a handsome, witty Nobel Prize laureate in a hilarious conga line headed straight for the swimming pool! (A party activity much missed from Peter Sellers movies of the seventies.) We'd end our evening together on a wistful note (we have others in our lives). However, the fact that I somehow network my way to a prestigious and well-paying job ("Call Marta in Santa Monica," he'll murmur. "She needs someone tomorrow!") that can be done from home, part-time, dims the pain.

So I drove to West Hollywood with a synthetic eagerness. The address turned out to be a glamorous penthouse with muted track lighting over quasi-museum objects, a faux-granite sink in the bathroom, and an all-white kitchen. Even the oven was white. Uh-oh, I thought. Red alarm lights were flashing in my head: Category 1! Category 1! What on earth had I been thinking, dragging along a Trader Joe's $1.99 Pinot like a slutty date? Surely $4.99 could have been parted with without too much effort. Even $6.99, $8.99! At $8.99, I might not have peeled off the price tag—I might just have "forgot"—leaving it there for all to see.

Beyond was a dining room with a well-laden food table. Impressive, since it appeared that no person had ever stirred a saucepan within these walls. I glimpsed rich swirling pastas, basil, pesto, tomatoes, all manner of crumbly cheeses. . . .

Eureka! I thought. I can hide my chintzy wine in that ethnic vase over there (Peter Sellers would) and make my way to Nirvana. I had found my party activity: eating. (A decent scavenger hunt, complete with prizes, appears to be too much to ask of these "adult" parties.) Hurrah for catering!

But then I saw them. Said Italian ricotta cheese-fest was flanked by one of my least favorite garnishes: a deadly ring of twenty-three-year-old, five-foot-eight-inch-and-taller size sixes and size fours, in skintight jeans and minis. These exceptionally fit and taut young women laughed and tossed their salon-fresh hair, unleashing rivulet after rivulet of Model Talk.

Now, I have nothing against models. I like them! I like them fine. Let them work and live well. L.A. is a great melting pot: there's no reason models, reformed gang members, convicted felons, and I shouldn't share our freeways in harmony. But I tell you, I don't like laughing models circling my Italian food in an unholy phalanx. Food they have no intention of touching. Why couldn't they go laugh in the foyer? Sigh. I poked an arm forward to grab a plate, but lost my nerve.

You see? The moms of my kindergarten class would never have allowed such a gloomy moment. Not Mrs. Anderson, Mrs. Cobb, Mrs. Chivukula, in their striped sixties mom dresses with their big friendly arms. "Come on, kids, come on," I see them eternally beckoning as they hand out plates and cups of milk. "Put on your Snoopy party hat and dig in! Who-o-o-o wants ice cream?"

So there! Until we bring my Dream Team party hosts back, I'm staying home. Just call me a big old . . . party pooper.

The Call
of the Wild

Living indoors can be absolutely exhausting.

A few weeks ago, I was lying atop our Spring Air Four Seasons Tri-Lumbar pillow-top bed, encased in two-hundred-thread deep-pocket percale sheets, reversible comforter, and matching goose-down pillows (regular and king-size). The whole thing stands about six feet high—you have to sort of run and vault to get into it. It was about midnight, and, as usual, I couldn't sleep.

First of all, I was hot. I felt like some kind of dumpling. Why do we have all this bedding anyway, I thought, kicking it off in a sudden frenzy. Because we'd wandered into Strouds Linen Warehouse, of course, and gone totally mad. But this is California—now I have to run the air-conditioning even in the winter!

Too exhausted by our bed even to pick up a book and read, I aimed the remote control at the TV. But it was the wrong remote control. We have seven. Some appear to be hand-me-downs from other people, other televisions, other technologies entirely. The TV looked tiny and distant. Even more distant, I knew, was the refrigerator, which cradled, among other things, a half slice of blueberry cheesecake. Deep in the folds of the Wamsutta Fantasy EnormoBed, though, I was unable to lift myself.

"Mike?" I called out to my boyfriend. But he couldn't hear me. He was in the living room watching the Mike Miller Horror Cinema Showcase. That's how he copes with insomnia—by renting, zombielike, entire marathons of unwatchable films. And not from the nice Sherman Oaks Blockbuster, but from the sleazy corner video/liquor store run by hirsute males in boogie shirts and gold chains. Tonight's picker-uppers included *Hellraiser III, Carnival of Souls,* and, finally, *Repulsion,* by Roman Polanski.

Help!

Nature advocate Edward Abbey—a fan of things like twenty-day solo hikes—once wrote that he'd shoot a person before a snake. To his way of thinking, snakes are natural, whereas people are sort of puffy and wasteful and smelly and I can't recall what else. In any case, I'm sure that whenever Abbey felt himself nauseated by civilization, it was our faces that rose before him.

We were people who needed to be slapped in the face by Nature. We needed her to scold us, to send us to our rooms without dinner, to wrest our comics away. We were bad, bad adults, listless and doughy and slack. We needed Mother Nature to box us roundly about the ears. And I wouldn't have it any other way. Because I've always turned to Nature when it's time to be punished.

In college, for instance, I insisted on dating these lean, athletic Sierra Club types with Ph.D.s in organic chemistry, their can-do optimism leavened with little gristly streaks of passive aggression. Weekends became All About Rock Climbing! Metal carabiners were always being thrust at one; I was constantly being belayed, like a stricken head of beef cattle, against my will. One day I slipped and slid down one thousand feet of scree on my tailbone.

Talk about anal. You would not believe the incredible attention paid, on these dismal little trips, to where and how one would pass a bowel movement. Carry Out What You Carry In was the motto. What we'd carried in was stringy beef Ramen and powdered Jell-O; over the rest, memory draws its gentle curtain.

"Bagging peaks" was the obsession of one bachelor. We'll call him Stan, because today I think he's actually head of some kind of multimillion-dollar particle accelerator. I imagine he has some frightened little family by now ("Dad says, 'Let's all climb Half Dome without ropes!'"), and his blood pressure is up to a thousand or his pulse is down to forty or whatever.

At any rate, in his formative years Stan's hobby was to write letters to the Sierra Club to keep them updated as to what new peaks he'd bagged over the weekend. Ever polite, they'd reward him with faint compliments and the occasional button. I'm sure the Sierra Club people were mumbling to each other, "What *is* it with this guy?" But Stan's thirst for the kind of recognition others might be more inclined to avoid was unquenchable.

The nadir came when Stan was allowed into something with a name like Sierra Club Jugglers on Peaks (SCJP). Yes, Stan was a juggler *and* he played the lute *and* he liked to wear a tattered J. R. R. Tolkien–type cape to dorm parties, and—oh, it's all too horrible to mention. Anyway, after we'd climbed five thousand vertical feet to a summit, my job was always to take a photo of Stan . . . juggling on one leg. To me, the sight was as ghoulish as if he'd worn his underpants on his head like a hat.

Fortunately, today I am older and flabbier and understand that

I am a person of low achievement. And so, corporal punishment by Nature is much easier to come by.

Out in Nature, Mike and I run with the Winnebagos. Forget finger-chimney climbs of 5.6 difficulty.

Heck, just schlepping our stuff fifteen feet from the car to our KOA-approved fire ring is exhausting: the blue-and-white Winnebago tent you can stand up in; the American Camper propane cooking stove; the metal camping plates with their three separate areas for meat, vegetables, and potatoes; two king-size air mattresses. Then come the down sleeping bags, the insulated pads, the flapping rain tarps, the extra comforters, the toothbrush cases, boxes of Kleenex tissues (just to have in general).

Now we're ready for the really cool stuff—the stuff that makes life worth living. The twenty-five-dollar Big 5 night-table lamp powered by a single "D" cell battery. Camp pillows you can blow up in two minutes (soon you find you're blowing up everything except your date). A camp shower consisting of a plastic sack of water that pours down from a tree. An ingenious five-minute air-mattress pump that plugs into any automobile cigarette lighter! "Who would have thought of this?" we marvel. "It's incredible!" We blow up our king-size air mattresses and then deflate them, just so we can blow them up again.

Next morning comes the enervating task of making breakfast on the little propane cooking stove using the mini camp utensils and the mini camp bowls that fit into each other in their mini camp way. We have to slice everything with the 1½-inch blade on Mike's Swiss Army knife because we forgot the Braun knife set. There are eggs and cheese and onions and potatoes and sliced bacon and even buckwheat pancakes.

Boy, I'm thinking, it's going to take twenty minutes just to wash these dishes with my tiny bottle of mini camp soap!

"How did you sleep?" I ask Mike suddenly.

"Terrible!"

"Me, too!"

Ah, yes. In the sky up above us, a hawk wheels. We exchange steely, knowing looks. Nature is beginning to pummel us. What a harsh mistress she is.

Antidote
to Civilization

Where did I go on vacation last month?

OK, I admit it. After all, the telltale words are spelled out for all to see on my pitifully bloated Visa bill (it rolls its eyes, it belches, sweat breaks out on its forehead . . .).

Club Med. That's right. Club Med.

As a matter of fact, my boyfriend, Mike, and I *did* wear matching tennis visors the whole week. We *did* "shake our booties" to pool aerobics. We *did* squeeze into neon Body Glove wet suits for that requisite "Overweight American Gladiators" photo-op, and—get this—even some tentative discoing was undertaken. We did it all! And we'd do it again.

Let me say that taking vacations has not always come so effortlessly to me. My problem is twofold: One, I have the attention span of a tsetse fly. And two, pulling twenties out of my wallet makes me nauseous. It literally does. The summer vacation snapshots of yore show me squinting in the middle of saying things like "The shrimp buffet is *how* much?" or "Hon, did the guy say the snorkel cruise to Flamingo Island was extra or included?" or "Ten dollars a bottle? For suntan lotion? Forget it!"

It's not that I have a problem with fun. I can have fun until the cows come home. I'm laughing just thinking about having fun. But the cost! After all, at home I can play computer solitaire for hours at a time, sipping my glass of Diet 7-Up spiked with Gallo French Colombard, the Chieftains twanging on the (paid-for) stereo, dog (was free) in my lap. See how relaxing? And just pennies away.

But the Club Med vacation (a.k.a. "The Antidote to Civilization," a slogan that took on a more profound meaning as the week progressed) made a convert of me. Because at Club Med, one swift kick to the nuts of the credit card does it all. A straightforward $1,090 per person yields air, lodging, three buffets a day, sailing, windsurfing, scuba, tennis, even nightly shows. So what if those shows typically begin "And now, Randy the snorkel instructor will lip-sync Bob Dylan's *Blowin' in the Wind.*" I can see the "quality" stuff at home, after all.

And talk about easy to get to—our plane descended into hunched little Guamyas airport—from customs, it was but ten paces to our Club Med van. We and five other Club Med-ers were whisked away. Outside the van window, Mexico—a mirage of cacti, dust, Tecate Beer signs, pickup trucks, and roadside stands—flew by. Twenty breezy minutes later, Mexico ended and Club Med—veiled behind a long, curving drive, impregnable adobe walls, and a heavy wooden security gate—began.

The guard looked us over, and the gate swung open. One could almost hear a gong. Indeed, the vista bore an eerie resemblance to that twenty-four-hour-a-day judo island Bruce Lee faced in *Enter the Dragon*. Acres of unusually green lawn rose up around us. Strange music pulsed through the air. Could it be the funky early eighties hits of Abba and Wang Chung? Why, yes! We watched as hundreds of Caucasians in sweatbands and knee pads leaped and twisted after airborne soccer balls, softballs, basketballs, and volleyballs.

Having toured the pleasure compound, Mike and I ached to sink our teeth into some fun. Conveniently enough it was three P.M.—cocktail hour. Cash is no good at Club Med; drinks are to be had for colored beads. Good enough. "Where's the lady who will give us our beads?" I wondered, palm outstretched hopefully.

In retrospect, I don't know what I was thinking. Obviously, if cocktails were free at Club Med, you could just walk up to the bar. But no. While I looked away, teeth clenched, trusty Mike peeled back two twenties for a big bag of beads ("grande"). He quickly fashioned them into a necklace—which shrank to a choker after two piña coladas. My bowels turned to ice.

"Oh, my God, at eighty-eight cents per yellow bead and forty-five cents per orange, we've just hurled away, what, twelve dollars?" I wailed. "For twelve dollars, we could have bought one whole bottle of Captain Morgan Spiced Rum at the Van Nuys Lucky." I opened my mouth in Edvard Munch's *The Scream*. But two sudsy piña coladas eased the pain.

And soon the spending of the vacation money lapsed into its usual dull rhythm. When the cash ran out, tired Mr. Visa was whipped out to do his duty. Anyway, I came to see good points about the beads. Sometimes a brunette in a halter top would execute a lusty volleyball serve, and those beads would just fly off into the sand. A deft eye could spot them later.

Meanwhile, there was the endless parade of food to be dealt with. Mayonnaise salmon, Mexican papaya, grilled steak, chicken tacos, Black Forest cake, french fries—maybe these foods didn't go together, but I managed to mound them on my plate nonetheless. You had to. It was a jungle out there. There were lines of ten or twelve people to get to the good stuff. Senior citizens, killingly expert from their many cruises, would cut in front of you at the creamed shrimp.

As you can imagine, by day two my aggressive instincts were strung out to the max. Whereas at home you can rarely coax me off the couch, at Club Med I became Ms. Volley Pal! I saw that beach, I felt that sun, and I was literally struck with Volley Fever.

Sadly, so were the many Club Med children whose parents did not want to see them for a few hours. Ten-thirty beach volleyball drew mostly the four-feet-and-under crowd, fumbling over the sand in their tennis shoes. Only I, Ms. Volley Pal, resplendent in my $16 Bullock's bathing suit, towered above, much like Goldie Hawn might in some hilarious summer movie. But the hilarity soon waned. No child was so tiny that he did not insist on playing middle blocker. I had to keep pushing them away from the ball.

Exhausted, I could see nothing for it but to ingest another three-thousand-calorie lunch. Then, big as whales, Mike and I found ourselves sucked inevitably toward the pool area for the daily "Sun Dance." Oddly hypnotized, we found ourselves moving our hips in rhythm with two hundred fellow Club Med-ers— hairy-chested dads in baggy shorts, sunscreen-slathered moms, newlyweds in matching bike shorts, children with wet hair. Motley as we were, for this one moment we moved as one, singing:

Don't blame it on the sunshine
(sweep arms in air)
Don't blame it on the moonshine
(vertical pointing)
Don't blame it on the good times
(pelvic thrusts)
Just blame it on the boogie!
(step right and circle hands)

Indeed, by this point there was an almost insurmountable load of things to be blamed on the boogie. "Do you think it was like this in Jonestown?" Mike whispered wonderingly, eyes glazed, in mid–pelvic thrust. I had no answer. All I knew was I'd probably try grape Kool-Aid . . . if it were included.

Tahiti!

"I'm old, I'm fat, I'm going to Tahiti."

Gauguin thought it, Brando thought it, and last month it was my turn. True, those guys were older when it hit them. Then again, they weren't surrounded by today's new breed of Frighteningly Clever Twenty-something Interns.

I mean, here I am going on thirty-three, logging fourteen-hour days, getting nowhere, and then I'm told by twenty-one-year-old Shien that I'm always clicking this wrong thing on Windows. Shien makes $8 an hour. Next, a slim, flannel-shirt- and nose-ring-wearing twenty-three-year-old named Nina leans in and corrects my spelling of "portentous." I thought it was "portentious." I don't know why.

Then they all flounce off to a West African djimbe concert. What is djimbe? Some hip KCRW thing, no doubt. Help! They are Stepford Interns, after my job. Which they can do better than me! Than I! What I *want* to tell them is: "Stop rocking the vote and start brewing my friggin' coffee! One day your arm fat, too, may fall!" Except I can't, because then Shien might modify my autoexec.bat file.

"Tahiti," I announce icily instead. "I'm going to take my vacation next week in Tahiti."

Tahiti, I've always felt, is the most offensive of the South Sea islands. It has no socially redeeming qualities. A topless little vixen of an island is Tahiti. Fiji, the Cook Islands, New Caledonia—all these seem intellectually complex by comparison. Even the Hawaiian Islands have become, well, oddly driven. These days, one is always four-wheeled to the back of Maui to see acres of aggressively tilled sugar cane. The University of Hilo has a U.S.-dominating women's volleyball team. *Manoa* is Hawaii's award-winning literary magazine. This is the new, brisk, forward-looking Hawaii, one senses, and everyone better get with it.

But Tahiti has been languishing lo these many years under the laconic hand of the French. Tahiti seems to do nothing but lie in a hammock in her teeny grass skirt, buff her nails, and snap, "Oh, merde," when she splits one. And I l-l-like that. It's very 1803, very Golden Age of Vacations. I suddenly want to go, "Argh! Me blarney leg!" and fall headfirst into a keg of rum. (Thus reenacting, I think, much of Tahiti's written history.) I may be totally wrong about this; these may be racist, sexist, imperialist comments. But . . . eat my shorts! I'm old, I'm fat, I'm going to Tahiti!

My fear was that people in Tahiti would not be old and fat enough. But when I arrive in Moorea, I cheer. Our Polynesian cab driver is unabashedly fat; she wears a lei; from the front seat protrudes the business end of a ukulele. Would my cruel friend Mel dare say to her, as he'd said to me: "Tahiti? And what size thong bikini are you going to wear? Large, medium, or the *stinger*?"

Why, I could be queen on this fertile island, I think exultantly. My cellulite would be sacred! "Sandra's thighs have swelled from a size ten to a size fourteen!" the natives would bellow to each other through conch shells. "Time for a celebration . . . and a feast of sweet, roasted pig!"

Tahiti has beaten even its Club Med into a kind of torpor. I always insist on Club Med. When I go on vacation, I demand to step from the plane, be handed an umbrella drink, and fall face first onto the sand. Club Med provides that, but their many activities can sometimes intrude; every other hour you have to run and hide from hairy Giancarlo the water-ballet instructor.

Mexico's Club Meds (where airfare is cheap, the water brisk) feature vigorous Seattle newlyweds in neon visors, high-fiving. By contrast, among Moorea's bungalows float bag-eyed French folk with barely the will to suck smoke from their cigarettes. They look like they've been disco dancing since 1984 and now wish to curl up in the fetal position on the sand and die.

But as the week evolves, I find myself bonding more and more with the French. You have to—just to escape the Australians. Before, I had no mental picture of Australia; now I understand it is much like a bowling alley in New Jersey, but bigger and with kangaroos. At our first dinner, a Sydney woman with huge frosted hair who is sawing her way through island-clubbed veal shrills: "The new Miss America— she's deef! Absolutely deef! She dit'in even know she won. 'Ow she's going to 'andle all 'er duties and responsibilities, I dunno!"

At least she likes us. The next night we sit with Ted, a DJ from Auckland, New Zealand. He is not at all intrigued by me and my boyfriend when we're introduced, respectively, as a writer and jazz musician from L.A.

"I say, any other Kiwis here?" Ted asks distractedly, neck craning about like a gazelle's. A DJ from Phoenix, Arizona, finally sparks his interest; they exchange business cards and network loudly.

By Thursday, conversation is meaningless anyway. Moorea is amazing, but after a lot of rum all tropical islands start to look alike: Vietnam in *Apocalypse Now*. The lone movie showing on our forty-seven-mile-perimeter paradise: *Beethoven's 2nd*, in French. Even the chefs go stir-crazy, making salmon in vanilla sauce with island beets and Chinese-style tortellini.

There is nothing to do, finally, but be fat. Rubenesque matrons drop their tops, the "Ooh" plopping out of their "la la's." Sixty-four-year-old Dutch businessmen drift by in pareos, bellies bared, hibiscus behind each ear. Then there is leathery Wayne from Vancouver—Dennis Hopper in an ACAPULCO! visor. How long has Wayne been on vacation? "A year," he murmurs through chapped lips. A year? "Certain mistakes" had been made at home, he relates, intense bright eyes darting, so he wanted to "get away from it all." Three months have been spent wandering in Costa Rica, "for the tranquility and the animals." Now it's on to Australia. Why? Leaning forward, he whispers: "Because I want to hold . . . a koala bear."

Koala bears everywhere will want to run for their lives; on the other hand, Wayne is carrying Visa and American Express. And if you have those, your paradise usually will find you.

Coming Home to Van Nuys

It can be hard, sometimes, to come home to Van Nuys.

Especially via LAX, when you've just gotten off the plane from New Mexico or Minnesota or some other faraway place where pale green cornfields shiver under a cobalt sky. . . .

So unlike Airport Parking Lot C, really, where Burger King debris sucks up around your ankles and rows and rows of battered automobiles sulk beneath an oily sun. You step over a smashed Michelob bottle and suddenly you remember your life: you're poor, you're anonymous, and you drive a shitty car.

You think about the scenic drive ahead, deep into the Grid of the sweltering Valley, home of a hundred King Bear Auto Centers, a thousand Yoshinoya Beef Bowls, and ten thousand yard sales, some consisting of no more than a couple of "Disco Lady" T-shirts flung out on a scabrous lawn like some kind of SOS. You want to close your eyes and say, "There's no place like home." But, in fact, you *are* home.

On my last return to L.A., the mantra I put to myself as I wandered the grim expanse of Parking Lot C, looking for my 1973 VW with its bad clutch, was: "What do I love about Van Nuys? What do I love about Van Nuys?" Twenty minutes later, when I found the car (in section Ss), I had an epiphany.

What's great about living in Van Nuys is that we, uh . . . we have a pretty good variety of take-out. Maybe that doesn't sound like much, but it's something they sure don't have in Minnesota.

And besides, we're talking a whole world of take-out possibilities. My kitchen drawer is bursting with menus that must have been hurled onto my front porch in the dead of night. Within five minutes of my house I can get at least a dozen different kinds of "ethnic" food—including 100 percent authentic soul food, Thai, Chinese, Salvadoran, East Indian, Northern Italian, Spanish (the chef is from Barcelona, not Mexico), Israeli, Cajun, German, and Japanese.

Ah, yes. You're imagining the vivid cadences of exotic languages. The bustle of wonderful bazaars and open-air markets full of kiosks, and street cars, and flapping geese, and bicycle bells. French guys with fresh baguettes roller-skating in Gene Kelly pants, mariachi music, an honest cobbler from Istanbul, and a very wise man from Tibet who can tell you everything about yaks.

The problem, of course, is that this joyous melting pot doesn't describe Van Nuys at all. Walt Disney never made it over here to redecorate. The notion of "ethnic charm" is a hoary old Americanism from the seventies. There are few vibrant ethnic enclaves in the Valley; what I didn't tell you is that for each nationality I've named, there is exactly one restaurant. One. Marooned by itself in a tiny strip mall, generally sandwiched between an X-rated video store and a Sally for Nails salon. Not all of them do very well.

The take-out places that do flourish here are ones that dispense terrific food at terrific speed. At one of my favorites, Golan Restaurant, the employees wear perpetual scowls as they hurl peppers and falafel into paper bags with deadly urgency. And the folks at Thai Koon Café, another find, do a mean delivery—clocking in at something like twelve minutes from their door to mine—no doubt having knocked down a few Domino's delivery guys on the way.

More common are the ethnic restaurants that are slowly dying on the vine. They have a certain lost quality I can identify with. No one seems to understand what they're doing here. It is the way of the Grid.

One example. About three years ago an Egyptian restaurant opened in a strip mall not far from here. And I don't mean your generic Middle Easternish Pita Hut chain. I mean *Egyptians*. I'm not sure if this place ever had a name. The location's previous take-out tenant was a Chicken Delight franchise, and the sign, featuring a startled yellow bird, remained up for a while even though the Egyptians didn't sell chicken. Nor was there much cause for delight; the place was always empty. You could see the young cook through the window, sitting by himself in an orange plastic chair, smoking cigarettes, reading the paper.

About two months later, suddenly a crudely lettered sign that simply read KABOB went up. Still nothing. Soon after, the management decided to abandon the idea of using English at all; KABOB came down, and energetic banners in Arabic flew up around the windows.

It was at this point that I really became interested. (I'm the worst kind of consumer: small income and exacting standards. You have to do a lot to get my attention, because when I let go of twelve dollars, I don't do it lightly.) Aha! I thought. They're only communicating with their own people. Something really fabulous must be going on.

But still the masses failed to flock. Why wasn't the Egyptian community (wherever it was) catching on to this? An eager visit to the restaurant revealed the answer. The authentic Egyptian-food experience turned out to be an overpriced (paper) plate of stringy beef, instant rice, and runny tomatoes. Three more dollars earned you a trip to the salad bar—featuring Lady Lee peas, which the cook poured expressionlessly from the can. They made a gentle splattering sound as they slid into the copious salad-bar vat.

What inspires some folks to relocate halfway around the world to the San Fernando Valley in order to feed bad food on paper plates to their own people? Perhaps the chef really did not want to be in the food industry at all. Perhaps his family pushed him into it, like my own Chinese father pushed me to be an aeronautical engineer. (He believed I was destined to shine in the Advanced Tactical Weapons Division at Hughes Aircraft Company. He was wrong.)

But the take-out place that makes me feel the worst is the one in the strip mall on my corner—the home of Royal India. I've come to know the owner; his name is Shah. Unfortunately, I've also come to know his troubles. Like many Indian restaurants languishing in the Valley, the food is in-credible: there's rich vindaloo, tikka masala like red paint, lamb sag delicately aromatic in its gleaming metal dish. The interior, too, is embarrassingly classy for a place flanked by an "All-Nite" liquor store. There are white tablecloths, napkins stuffed in wineglasses like bouquets, and two bow-tied waiters who speak in perfectly modulated British accents. And it's going out of business. It kills me. I want to write the owner a note:

> Dear Shah, I can't afford to spend twenty-five dollars on dinner every night, but I want to keep you in my neighborhood. You are a culinary genius. I wish I could help!

But I don't. Instead, I slide another frozen dinner into the microwave. One block away, Shah peers out of Royal India's red curtains, watching for invisible customers on what is called Victory Boulevard. Up above him, a neon COIN LAUNDRY sign blinks on and off.

On the California Riviera

Until recently, I didn't know we *had* a "California Riviera." Then again, I live in Van Nuys, home of a Lucky so bedraggled one can't seem to escape without a soggy lettuce leaf attached to the bottom of one's shoe. We're pretty far from the Pacific Ocean here, and all the glitter that goes with it.

"They want to sell *us* beachfront property?" I asked my friend Duncan incredulously, poring over the map he'd been sent by the Riviera Beach & Spa Resort. The resort couldn't be more than a mile from Dana Point, a place I'd heard described as quite glamorous indeed. "And it's right there," I marveled, "smack in the middle of the California Riviera! It can't be possible!"

But it was. The recession, I deduced, must be having its effect on the luxury home market. All the Riviera people wanted to know was that we made thirty-five thousand dollars a year. We didn't; and yet I understood, in a vague theoretical way, that even thirty-five thousand dollars a year generally didn't spell beachfront property in Southern California.

"Not that they're struggling," Duncan said. "The woman on the phone said they're selling like wildfire."

Still, they wanted to talk. If Duncan and I would just take time out from our busy schedules for a two-hour tour, we were guaranteed to win: (1) a 1993 Jeep Grand Cherokee (retail value, $27,000); or (2) $10,000 in cash; or (3) Exotic Club Med Vacation (retail value, $2,495); or (4) Tropical Hawaiian Holiday (retail value, $667); or (5) $500 Broadway shopping spree; or (6) Sony 20-inch color TV with remote (or $350 in cash) in the "Luxury Lifestyles . . . Multi-Million-Dollar Bonanza!"

"Riviera!" I enthused, as we winged our way down the 405. L.A.'s auto dealerships and card casinos began to fall away, revealing Orange County's rolling green hills, snaking lines of Kaufman-and-Broad-style mansions in regulation eye-pleasing pastels, and beyond, the sparkling blue face of the Pacific. "Dana Point!" I shrieked. "The California Riviera! We're here!"

We looked at the map. No, we weren't quite there. The Riviera still lay ahead. "OK," said Duncan, foot to the gas. All at once the road hopped over to the right. The strip of sand that was the beach became narrower, dingier—a twisted Quasimodo-like shoulder of what it had been before. Even the ocean seemed to turn gray. To the left of the highway, without enthusiasm, rose a mud-brown cliff. Hunched in a seam between cliff and road— practically banging their elbows against each other—were cramped condos, liquor stores, fish shanties.

"This can't be right," Duncan puzzled. "According to the address numbers, we've already passed it."

I felt dismay. How could we have missed a resort so huge?

How, indeed. RIVIERA BEACH & SPA RESORT, read the brave

blue sign in front of the first set of cookie-cutter condos we'd passed. Faces ashen, we pulled into the "Reception Area," a garage veined with pipes and cables. Grim valets took the car.

"Hello! I'm . . . Nanci!" A plump, tan woman of thirty-five with a blonde feathered haircut, white polo shirt, and blue pants motored toward us. Her enthusiasm blazed ghoulishly against the dank environment. "Welcome to the Riviera Beach & Spa Resort! It's gorgeous here, isn't it?"

"This can't be happening," I whispered.

"Think *prizes*," Duncan hissed, pushing me forward.

Rather than just show us the resort, Nanci seemed eager to know us, draw us out. "I love the beach, don't you?" she asked cheerily, nudging us up a dingy stairwell. "Have you tried Jet Skiing? I'm absolutely addicted to Jet Skiing!"

"They Jet Ski here?" I asked, thinking of the gray ocean.

"Jet Ski, bodysurf, sunbathe, jog," Nanci rattled off. "Duncan!" She turned swiftly, flipping her hand outward as though introducing a fascinating new conversational topic. "You're a hard-working man. How often would you say you enjoy a 'minivacation'? Three, four times a week?" As it turned out, Nanci's idea of a minivacation was taking a dip in one of the Riviera's Jacuzzis.

The minivacation was the first of many difficult-to-grasp concepts Nanci presented to us. The second was the desirability of our location. "I just love to stand out here," she confided, as she led us to a covered balcony. Behind us, two teenagers in oversize pants played Ping-Pong, thundering about on the echoing cement floor. Unperturbed, Nanci rolled her head. "Feel that sun. And look over there." Her eyes popped open. "Dana Point!"

The three of us gazed along the trajectory of her finger, which swept past: (1) tour buses full of seniors; (2) roaring highway; (3) chain-link fence; (4) railroad tracks; (5) parking lot; (6) thin strip of beach scattered with metal garbage cans—toward a hazy land mass beyond.

"You've heard of Dana Point, haven't you?" Nanci asked. "You can go there for luxury shopping. They have a Delaney's and an El Torito," she mentioned casually.

Guest amenities actually on the Riviera premises consisted of two Jacuzzis, a tiny pool overlooking the highway, exercise equipment, and a game room. The latter was closetlike; a lone employee sat guard, reading the paper. Behind him, the game room amenities included: (1) stacked beach chairs; (2) beach balls; (3) many, many sets of Parcheesi.

The climax of the tour, though, was the Riviera Beach & Spa Resort video, hosted by Mr. Luxury himself, Robin Leach. "The California R-r-riviera!" he exclaimed, r-r-rolling his Rs, his scant hair flying in the breeze. "Why do Californians spend so much money traveling to places like Hawaii?" he mused, in a kind of wonderment. "Look at the great vacation values right here—at a fraction of the cost!"

Why indeed? Because one week a year at the Riviera Beach & Spa Resort—including, admittedly, all the Parcheesi you can handle—costs seventeen thousand dollars (seven years of easy $310 monthly payments). That's right—the Riviera is a condo timeshare "opportunity." So what if you're not guaranteed the same unit each year so you can't even hang a picture in "your" condo? You have Jacuzzi minivacation privileges all year long!

"And remember, that's for *life*!" Nanci pleaded as we shook our heads no. We were sympathetic, but we had our own concerns. Like figuring out how to make use of our prize: five free nights' lodging in Hawaii! Unfortunately, we'd have to spring for our airline tickets, rent our car, and buy our meals.

Still, we felt bad for Nanci, as we looked at the cramped pool one last time. She wasn't taking this well. Did she own here?

"Yes, I do," Nanci replied, still tearful at our rejection. "I love it so much I actually bought in for *two* weeks a year. It's the only place I know of where you can sit in a Jacuzzi and look at the sea at the same time," she said, her eyes fixed on the Pacific while children screamed and traffic roared by.

Christians Reconsidered

All right, single girls, listen up: Have I got a blind date for you! I'm serious. He's thirty-three, tall, handsome, athletic, smart, generous, gainfully employed, and socially progressive (e.g., he gives away a third of his income to charity). He's never been married and has no bad habits. Doesn't even fart! I should know: he's my brother.

There's just one thing. He's a . . . a Christian.

"Oh, no!" exclaimed one of my artist friends in horror upon hearing this. She shook her dangly ethnic earrings as if to ward off a vampire—a response typical of the card-carrying bohemoisie. Shove the most grisly Mapplethorpe in her face and she yawns. Suggest she date a nice Christian fella and she freaks.

Not that I don't understand where she's coming from. Christianity today has a bit of a PR problem: you have manic depressives in rainbow wigs flashing John 3:16 at baseball games. You have UHF shows featuring weepy Tammy Faye look-alikes, white pianos under chandeliers, and flashing 976 numbers. The occasional murder or hostage-taking continues to be a sore spot.

Even Christians who aren't technically felons can make a person uncomfortable. I remember the time I went out with Jeff, a cute guy I met in college. We were halfway through a lovely Thai dinner; we had discussed the music of John Coltrane; we had discovered a common love of volleyball. Our faces were flushed. Lanterns swayed hypnotically.

Grasping my hand, Jeff impulsively leaned forward. "Sandra?"

"What?" I asked huskily.

"Have you accepted the Lord Jesus Christ as your savior?"

Just like that. No warm-up. No mood music. No idle teasing around the God issue to loosen the soil. Had Jeff grabbed my breast I would not have been more shocked. Because I, for one, find that question terribly rude. Religion is deeply personal and complex. One's views cannot always be captured in a simple yes or no answer:

"Yes, but I think homosexuals are OK and the Rapture is hooey," or "No, but I pray and somehow find myself going to church on Sundays." And that's the quarrel I have with even some nice, middle-of-the-road Christians. Their constant administering of this pass/fail test can terrify and stifle.

The strange thing was, I *had* accepted Jesus. But mine wasn't exactly the kind of story one likes to tell over and over again.

My bout with religion occurred during the mid-seventies—an era of macramé vests, bell-bottoms, and the music of Andrew Lloyd Webber. (Remember those thrilling chords "*Je*-sus Christ! *Su*-per Star!") My *Living Bible* dazzled with its pop art and flowered cover. *Godspell* productions ran rampant; fresh-faced young Up With Jesus members dressed in striped overalls did the funky chicken as they told the parables of Matthew using hand puppets.

And here I was at age thirteen—at the peak of raging prepubescence—contemplating this. The psychedelia, my hormones . . . it was too much. In my mind, Mr. Jesus became but one of the many characters in that weird Freudian psychodrama called junior high.

"When the Rapture comes, Jesus is going to leave you behind!" I remember screaming at my parents, slamming the bedroom door. "And good riddance!"

My personal Christian doctrine was a cross between the Book of John and some cheesy adolescent story called "Sandra Loh: Teen Evangelist!" I can't explain why, but much of this fantasy centered around the prom. My idea was that the most popular ninth-grade boy would be drawn to me because I wasn't slutty. Somehow I'd wind up going to the prom and making a convert all in one evening—while the non-Christian girls looked on jealously. (And why not? I'd be wearing my cute go-go boots and my hair would be perfect.)

It couldn't last, of course. My expectations of Christianity were terribly high. So high I was bound to be disappointed, again and again. "I'll hear bells when I'm a Christian!" I thought. "I'll fly like a kite!"

And yet there I sat, still in my room, my algebra book open in front of me, my dull family moving about outside my door. Why was this not working? Maybe I had not *really* accepted Jesus right the first time. Maybe I should do it again. I pictured Jesus on the cross, me on the ground, lousy with sin. I felt bad. Real bad. I squeezed out a tear . . . and listened hopefully. Where were the bells? They never came. Over the years I came to think *I* was the problem. Finally Jesus and I became embarrassed with each other and slunk off to our respective corners.

Sigh. Every so often I wonder if God looks down and cringes. There He is, hovering in the blue sky over the Sierras, a thoughtful Emersonian type who enjoys a fine wine and loathes polyester. (With apologies to feminists, I still see Him as a He. When I picture God as a female I see this heavyset woman of fifty hoeing in Topanga.) The Almighty may well look down and see a GOD IS MY COPILOT bumper sticker and think, "Ouch." He may well look at Andres Serrano's new twist on the crucifix and think, "Yow! No art funding for *him* in his next life," before moving briskly *on*.

If God is this reasonable a being, I got to thinking recently, I might actually enjoy having invisible conversations with Him. I'd seek His counsel on those icky moral questions of the nineties (e.g., should I give the scraggly looking white couple on my doorstep six dollars because their car broke down, or is this a scam? If it is, should I care? How much money per hour can they make this way, anyhow?).

So one Sunday I decided to accompany my brother to church. Why not? Now that I'm an adult, I thought, maybe I should give spirituality another try. My brother's scientific brain had not yet exploded from contact with organized religion, hence neither would mine. Shocking as it was to consider, it was entirely possible that Pat Buchanan *wouldn't* even be there.

On the morning in question the postcard-perfect California sun fell over everything, the sky was crystalline, eucalypti shimmered. Nary a police siren or car alarm could be heard. It made me feel great to be alive. It made me think: Isn't it amazing that humans really like blue and there's so much of it above us? Could this be a *coincidence*?

"Hello!" my brother and I said to the pleasant reverend at the door. "Hello!" we said to the nice elderly couple giving out programs.

But then I saw them. Standing before the altar were the *Godspell* people—the same eerily cheerful faces I remembered from my teenage years, the same I-feel-like-chicken-tonight dance movements. I felt a wave of nausea. One member wielded a badly tuned guitar while they sang:

Jump for joy!
Jesus Christ is living!
Jump for joy!
Jesus Christ is Lord! Woo!

Nope. This wasn't for me. Christianity, maybe. Jesus-jumping, no. Shaking my head, I looked over at my brother. And to my surprise, he looked slightly pained. What's this? My brother embarrassed? Could it be?

On the other hand, why had I assumed he'd like *Godspell*? So "Jump for Joy" was a rotten song—God didn't write it. It dawned on me: Maybe you could hate *Godspell* and still be a Christian. Wow. Maybe this tent was a lot bigger than I thought.

Intrigued, I lifted a hymnal from the rack in front of me. As I did so, a memory flashed: Christmas 1965. Through the glow of candles I saw my Chinese father seated in a pew, his head bowed over his chest, an occasional snore escaping him. Meanwhile, my German mother, in an odd lace hat that looked like a pancake, belted out "Silent Night" as though she'd been there.

For better or worse, what a familiar place the Christian church is. It's a place I remember from childhood, a place I drop in on as an adult, a place I love, a place I hate, a place I argue with my brother about. But for me, no matter how silly the church's trappings sometimes seem, the mystery of religion continues to intrigue.

White
Trash

There are some L.A. addresses so unfashionable that people actually recoil in horror when you admit you live there. West Covina is up there, along with Torrance. People sense that some dreaded brush with reality has put you in such a place and that a depressing story will follow. A story like "My uncle owns a duplex in Sylmar. After he broke his hip, I moved in to give him a hand—I wasn't making any money writing spec scripts anyway. Now my job is to rent the top unit to recent immigrants and replace the light bulbs. And you know what? I like it!"

And of course, no basin puts people off as much as the San Fernando Valley. The feeling is absolute. The same people who'll drive from Santa Monica to Pasadena (twenty-five miles) without blinking find lunch in Reseda (sixteen miles) much too far. Almost dangerously far. It's a weird magnetic thing, having to do with going the wrong way up the 405.

On the other hand, there's a certain liberating quality to living so far out that no one wants to bring pot luck to your dinners.

Take the time I spent living in Winnetka. Where the hell is it? You take the 101 north out of Hollywood. You eventually veer west, hit the 405, and—here's the kicker—you keep going! The off-ramps for Reseda, Tarzana, and Winnetka ring out like a kind of lonesome cowboy refrain.

Our three-bedroom house—located on Winnetka Boulevard within hollering distance of the orange CANOGA PARK MOTOR INN/CANOGA PARK BOWL revolving sign—was your basic West Valley tract home. Built in the sixties, it boasted the materials of its time: stucco, aluminum, "sunburst" linoleum, Formica, brown ocher shag carpeting.

So what? It was cheap . . . and we had a pool! So the pool was made of gray cement with an AstroTurf diving board. So it was surrounded by a chain-link fence and weeds. So it wasn't heated. The San Fernando Valley can be a good ten to fifteen degrees hotter than the rest of Los Angeles; in the summer that sucker would climb up over ninety degrees. *Sploosh!* (And then you'd hear: Arf, arf, arf, arf, arf! That, of course, would be our woolly Australian shepherd, Joey, now soaking wet—and furious—after someone had cannonballed him.)

But the most beautiful thing about Winnetka, I soon found, was that its sheer distance from town acted as a kind of social sieve. Would I go see a friend-of-a-friend's politically conscious rock band at ten-thirty P.M. at the Coconut Teaszer ($2-off tickets)? No, it was too far. Would I go to a meeting in Hollywood to help plan a fund-raiser for yet another struggling arts group? Gee, it was far. Could I make it to the USC class I was TA-ing by nine-thirty A.M.? Heck, it was just too far!

"Ha ha ha ha ha!" I'd shout, whizzing down the wobbly blue plastic slide. *Sploosh!* And then: Arf, arf, arf, arf, arf! I'd continue to splash, splash, splash Joey as he ran around the pool.

July came, and the sliding glass doors of the neighbors' stucco-and-aluminum faux ranch-style house opened. Aerosmith and Warrant began pumping from within. Nineteen-year-old girls with stringy hair, bikini tops, and jeans arrived in Toyota pick-ups. As for the male occupants of that house . . . you want white trash? It looked like the entire membership of ZZ Top was living next to us in their boxer shorts.

Our neighbor's tiny cement-lined, weed-fringed pool was technically a wading pool. And wade they did. The ZZ Toppers and their bikini girls flailed and fell heavily into the water as only people who are using their underwear as bathing suits can. At one point an actual *forklift* was driven in: a ZZ Topper would climb up on it and then, without expression, perform a resounding cannonball. I can still see the graceful flutter of his boxer shorts. *Sploosh!*

But the pièce de résistance came one 110-degree afternoon when our neighbor's pit bull clambered over the five-foot cement wall—all trembly legs and testicles—hovered for an agonizing second, and plunged into the pool like a ton of bricks. *Sploosh!*

"Oh, my God!" our friend Keith shrieked, trying to bat him away. The pit bull was surprisingly aquatic, pedaling through the water as if on a bicycle. My boyfriend, Mike, cannonballed in, trying to separate them. *Sploosh!* Then, hilariously, Joey was pushed into the pool, too. *Sploosh!*

When Joey managed to extract himself from the fray, he left the premises via a loose board in the gate. Just took off. Apparently, even our dog had had enough. The laughter dropped from our faces.

We had the sense that just maybe we'd drifted too far from civilization's moorings. Living so far from La Brea, maybe we *were* becoming Valley trailer-park people. Why, just the day before, our other neighbor—a fiftyish Latino professional who had the misfortune of being the only guy on the block who actually owned his house—had knocked on our door, asking bravely, "Could you please ask your friends to stop parking on the front lawn?"

I won't dwell too long on the nightmare that followed. "Joey, Joey!" we called for our errant dog, heartbroken, as we searched endless back alleys. And for the first time we saw all the other dogs in Winnetka. They whined at their own chain-link fences and scrabbled on their own cement patios. They were eager to do what Joey and even the neighbor's pit bull had done: They wanted out. Now!

What did they think was out there? Alaska? Surrounding them on all sides was the endless Grid of brown houses hunched behind balding lawns, and drive-in movie-theater screens thrust into the sky like dour monoliths.

Joey finally turned up in tony Tarzana (a.k.a. south of Ventura Boulevard). He arrived back *chez* us washed, brushed, coiffed, fluffed, and armed with a big green bow. He'd been hiding out with a Christian couple who kept calling him Monkey. They were barely able to release him to us.

"We don't *want* a reward," they said through clenched teeth. "Just fix that gate, will you? My Lord!"

Today, of course, I wouldn't splash Joey for an entire six-pack of Labatt's. He sits approvingly with me now, under the desk as I type at the computer, return phone calls, pay bills, and do all the other things that make the days look alike. We live *east* of the 405 now—a different ballgame entirely. But sometimes during the hottest San Fernando Valley afternoons, if I listen hard enough, I think I can hear a distant . . . *sploosh!*

Daddy Dearest

I insist that this be the last column about my father. OK, maybe I've never actually written a whole column about him before, but I don't want this to become a habit. Understand that for years anecdotes about my father—what I thought were throwaways—were the only things anyone would remember about me. There I'd stand, one hip jutted out, bangs moussed up impressively, in my black turtleneck and beret, waving a wineglass and arguing heatedly about the potential impact of technology on performance art. I realize now that . . . well, no one cared. They wanted funny stories about my Chinese father.

Recently I ran into Paul, an experimental video-maker I'd known—almost intimately—in the mid-eighties. We convened at our host's cheese platter.

"I've been wondering for year . . ." he murmured, resting a hand lightly on my arm.

"Yes?" I breathed.

All at once a flame leapt into his eyes, his face contorting with glee. "How's your dad? Does he still wear his underwear backward and do the Chinese snake dance on Pacific Coast Highway?"

I closed my eyes in pain. No. Of course not. Well, yes.

First let us take a step backward. Forget *my* dad. Immigrant parents in general tend toward eccentricity, don't they? They arrive from the old country; then suddenly they have VCRs and Cuisinarts, their children are growing up to be monsters, and, worse, the local Ralph's stops carrying pig knuckles.

Nationality doesn't matter. My friend Fred's parents, who emigrated from France, have bathroom counters overflowing in dental floss. (They can't bear to part with anything that's been used only once.) And several years ago when Fred's cousin returned from a summer trip in London, he was greeted at the Greyhound bus station by the sight of Fred's mother waving an enormous British flag as she cried out, "Halloo! Halloo!"

Is my father really that much odder than the rest of his ilk? For the record, he does *not* wear his underwear backward. Only his sweaters. The idea is, when the elbows wear through, you just turn them around and keep going. And yes, he did perform the Chinese snake dance for us kids, naked, armed only with a fluttering beach towel as he leapt and twirled, imparting his ancient Chinese folk song with a mournful howl. (He wasn't on the PCH at the time, but what laws—physical or federal—may have been broken, I can't say.)

Still, Paul wasn't completely off the mark about the Pacific Coast Highway—Dad's lived in Malibu for some thirty years now, threatening to cause property values to tumble along with him. Once a neighbor called the police to complain that my father was hanging out his old, holey underpants to dry, Shanghai-style, on clotheslines strung out in front of the garage. Excited, my father took the moral high road: "You know what disgusts me? Their Mercedes—that symbol of American materialism! They park it on their driveway every single day!"

The complaint calls stopped, but questions remain: Does my father, a retired aerospace engineer with science degrees from Stanford, Purdue, and Cal Tech, *have* to wear holey old underpants? Is this a person who can afford, say, *new* underpants? And a Maytag dryer perhaps? Why, yes, would have to be my answer.

As with many other Hughes engineers circa 1963, my father bought his Malibu home for the then impressive price of $47,000. By now, of course, the mortgage has long since been paid off, and the property—laundry lines notwithstanding—has shot up in value. Further, my father is one of those furtive older people who have untold stocks, bonds, mutual funds, IRAs, and whatever else that they continually shift from one account to the next, even as they complain loudly about how a loaf of bread today can set you back $1.79. I have seen stacks and stacks of bank statements stuck into drawers, all rubber-banded together and wrapped tightly in little plastic Lady Lee sandwich bags.

I don't want to give the impression that my father is rolling in cash. After all, lawsuits are regularly hurled at him by his second (ex) wife—the hotheaded Chinese one he brought over from the mainland after a brisk, eerily cheerful exchange of letters and photos. Once here, Liu made it clear that her big ambition was to break into Hollywood. (As she spoke no English, Chinese folk singing was her "hook.") So maybe Liu did have unreasonable expectations of America. There was bound to be friction. On the other hand, I did side with her on the transportation matter. . . .

For as long as I can remember, my father has, uh, hitchhiked in and out of Malibu. (I ask you: When will it end? When will it end?) Yes, he owns a car (he even bought me one—a Hyundai; he had to shelter income). But driving is so wasteful. The RTD is terrific, but only runs about once an hour. Besides, he meets such nice people.

I have never actually seen him—at the corner of Wilshire and Fourth Street, let's say, clutching his Lucky grocery bag of scientific papers (why spend money on a briefcase?)—and not picked him up. That would be a little too "how sharp the serpent's tooth." But I have been tempted to press my foot against the gas and speed forward toward the Pacific, happy and free, like people whose seventy-year-old dads aren't still copping rides from the public.

"So I'm standing at the corner of Wilshire and Ocean, trying to flag a ride," he tells me grandly last week. (To him, all cars are potential cabs.) "It's a good spot, very visible."

"Uh huh," I say.

"And a beautiful, elegant lady in a Mercedes picks me up." (Mercedes are not quite so disgusting when they're giving him rides.) "And she looks familiar to me, very familiar."

I brace myself.

"She knows a lot about Bill and Hillary," my father rushes on. (Almost as much as he does, being his unspoken implication.) "She met them at the White House. We had a nice conversation about them. And then I say, 'I don't know much about the movies—but I know you! Can I get your autograph?" And she writes it for me, look."

> To Mr. Loh,
>> It was a pleasure to have you in my car.
>> Love,
>> Anjelica Huston
>> XXX

"Do you know her?" my father asks, beaming. "A very nice lady. She was very knowledgeable about Chinese opera and film," he chats airily. "Her father was the film director John Huston," he drops, in case I don't know this. Unlike Ms. Huston, I didn't go into my father's line of work, and this has always been a bit of a disappointment for him.

Then again, while Anjelica Huston was a good ride, she was not a dream ride. "She had another friend to drop off in Beverly Hills," he says, leaning in confidingly, looking a bit sad, "which took me a little out of my way. It would have been quicker for me to hop on the crosstown bus—I had a transfer—but by then . . ." He lowers his voice, an expert in such delicate matters of decorum, "I thought getting out might be a bit rude."

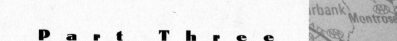

Part Three

Life in
the City

San Fernando
15
Sunland
12
Burbank
Hollywood
101
Studio City
West Hollywood
HOLLYWOOD BOWL
BLVD
SANTA MONICA BLVD
Century City
10
Culver City
SLAUSON
Inglewood
Lennox
Redondo Beach
Redondo Beach State Beach
Rolling Hills
VERDES DR
Royal Palms St. Beach

Bachelors
over Thirty

If a man isn't married by age thirty-six, he's doomed to live alone. True, when I came up with that theory I was twenty-six and in a bad mood. All urban females are cranky at twenty-six. Thirty is just seconds away, and everyone has turned against you. No one likes your demo tapes, no one thinks applying to med school is a good idea (given that your B.A. was in art history), no one is on your side about the modeling thing, an idea that flew into your head just yesterday.

During that Mad Year, my project was a guy we'll call Robert. He was perfect for me: thirty-three years old, a TV composer, tallish, most of his own hair, single. He'd just bought a lovely house in Glendale—fruit trees, small deck, even a nice utility room with pull-out ironing board. That was ideal, because if I don't iron stuff right when it comes out of the dryer, I tend to never get to it.

Robert was in Move-In Condition. The one problem? He was always kind of . . . tired. During dinner, yes, he'd be alert, animated, even flirtatious, in a general, targetless way. He'd make the right jokes, ask the right questions. But come nine P.M., Robert's attentive features would droop into a grimace of exhaustion. It was a look you never see on the faces of horny twenty-five-year-old guys, a look of terrible candor that said: "I can't bear another second of you and your ceaseless blabbering. Right now, there's nowhere in the world I'd rather be than home, watching CNN with my cat."

Robert, in short, had crossed that certain dark boundary within a man's soul. He'd entered into a place where fifteen minutes seems a long drive for dinner and a movie. Where he skips the predate shower in favor of a few swipes with the Speed Stick. Where all through dinner he's plotting how to beg off early before she asks that gonad-shriveling question: "Will you read my poems?"

Robert had reached the Bachelor over Thirty (BOT) plateau, where it's just not worth it anymore for ten minutes of middling sex. In ancient cultures, of course, we didn't have BOTs. Men married their two-hundred-pound second cousins at age eighteen, raised ten children, swung a hoe over tiny patches of brittle land, and died at twenty-eight.

The nineties, by contrast, are a time of wild experimentation. Not with regard to sex, but to men and women living for longer periods of time without each other. Prolonged bachelorhood, however, is not good for men or their health. Even in relatively young BOTs—thirty- to thirty-five-year-olds—you can notice the first twitches of creaky codgerhood. Take Paul, thirty-two. Single, cute, works in graphics, nice guy. Then you see him peel his orange at lunch. Clockwise, in circles, wipes his Swiss Army knife first on one side, then the other. He arranges the slices in a half-moon, eats right to left. Crumples the napkin, basket. It's a ritual. Call him on it and his face flames red; still, he quietly hunches, busily peeling, arranging.

"I was over at Larry's apartment the other day," says Anne, a worried older sister. The BOT in question is thirty-three. "On the chair by the front door was a . . ." Her voice drops to a whisper. "Shoehorn. He's started to put his shoes on with a *shoehorn*."

Scary, huh? Now consider the back story.

For three years now, Larry has been dating Debbie, a shy brunette with *fabulous* values. Larry's family loves Debbie. Debbie loves them. Larry thinks he loves Debbie, but he has what we'll call the Elle syndrome. He has Debbie on hold. He can't shake the feeling that at any moment he might be able to trade in the Debbie for an Elle MacPherson.

Never mind that Larry is five foot nine, has no chin, and is a man for whom "evening wear" denotes clean sweatpants. The relatively easy access modern male Homo sapiens have to the *Victoria's Secret* catalog has confused them. "Whoa—that Nikki," is all Larry can gurgle the morning after a party, "she was hot! Boy! Woo!" Nikki is always a twenty-two-year-old Venezuelan swimsuit model, six feet in heels, living with a bisexual rap producer. Larry is a slump-shouldered computer guy wielding a tiny shoehorn. When will L.A. men learn what guys in other cultures have known for centuries? You can't date a woman with breasts bigger than your head.

Yet Larry is a find compared with Bill, age thirty-eight. For all his faults, Larry has been known to clean his bathroom—that's right, actually scrub the bowl. Bill, on the other hand, is a playwright given to magnificent, three-day-long depressions: "Agenbite of inwit," he sighs, "Agenbite of inwit."

Sitting on the can and reading newspapers for hours (*Terror in Bosnia! Famine in Somalia!*) is typically how such remorse of conscience is handled. The only problem is that Bill then drops the pages onto the floor; there they remain for weeks, transforming his tiny Palms bathroom into what aghast visitors call "a kind of litter box." No wonder Bill now fixes females at parties with an unshaven glare, asking: "Do you want to go out with me or not? Spare us both the wasted time and misery and just say no."

Past forty, though, pressure releases. The wind rises once again; the bachelor frigate eases forward with full sails—either obsessively ironed or morosely tattered, as the case may be. By now, all the Debbies have married their Stan-the-surgeons (kids: Kelly and Kyle; house: Brentwood; schedule: aggressively mapped).

Not that Debbie is angry at Larry anymore. Quite the opposite. In fact, she and her family kindly fold weird "Uncle" Larry to their bosom over less important holidays. Clad in visor and floppy (but clean!) drawstring pants, our hero spends his afternoons golfing, fishing, going to the track. He can't believe Stan— a lean, mean fifty-four—has the energy to play two hours of tennis a day, go to the hospital, sleep with the wife, cook for the kids . . .

"Oof, my knees," Larry says, farting . . . perhaps, indeed, a kind of fart heard round the world.

Being
Single

Me, single, is not a pretty sight. I seem to lack the single gene—the one that enables adults to live alone decorously. For me, a fair amount of weeping is involved. There is the dismal sensation of rolling over in bed in the middle of the night and finding slippery, half-read *New Yorker* magazines stuck to one's thighs and chest. Soon even the daily ups and downs of the KCRW summer pledge drive ("Just one caller on the line? Just one?") begin to trigger major mood swings.

I *am* the pledge drive. And no one is calling.

I'm not *really* single, of course. Just temporarily abandoned by my live-in boyfriend of five years. The reason given was three months of high-profile, high-paying, career-making work abroad. At one point, I believe champagne glasses were actually clinked to celebrate.

So, I can't cook. So, I'm starving to death in his absence. What do couples do but gain weight together? Sure, eating fried-oyster-on-sourdough sandwiches in front of the TV at midnight is a hell of a lot of fun—perhaps the best one can hope for in this sorry life. "Ba-OOM-ba!" I and my beloved used to cry out, chubby satyrs in floppy pajamas, swinging our bellies together like timpani.

Just you and your fat—which is what Singlehood boils down to—is another story entirely. Where is the joy? I recently took my fat with me to a dinner party and found the experience quite discouraging. We huddled in a corner, white-knuckling a wineglass, watching the vivid ones:

In the middle of the room stood Jude, a poised, attractive thirty-four-year-old. She literally glowed with Singleness. She was informing the group about the new Isabel Allende book she'd read, the ending of which she found especially poignant. Not only was she starting books, she was finishing them! I and my fat found this absolutely amazing.

Our gaze traveled over the others. How well Singlehood was going for them. How groomed and fit they looked. How productive their weekends! No one at this dinner party ever paused at three on a Sunday afternoon, fingered her IKEA cactus, and sighed, ever so lightly, "Ah, me." These were industrious single people who grabbed their spare time to jog around the Hollywood Reservoir—perhaps with a screenplay buddy, batting about ideas like boxers.

But at ten-thirty P.M. something even more amazing happened. Like clockwork, all these Singles turned to get their coats! "Oh, well," they yawned. "Look at the time!" Apparently, no one was going to hang on until one A.M., "helping" the hostess stack dishes, angling for a third cup of decaf, the stench of desperation hanging like a cloud.

Then I understood. To these L.A. thirty-somethings, Single-ness wasn't a curse. It was a lilting "Song of Myself," sung daily. It said, "Yes!" to life. It said, "Better off on my own! No longer gonna play Sid to anyone's Nancy!"

Inspired, I went home to tend the keenly intelligent garden of my own Singleness. Like a patient farmer, I stacked Trader Joe's frozen dinners in my cart while humming the theme from *The Piano*. Blockbuster videos were harvested, Quality Paperback accounts drizzled with checks, phone calls to friends were planted, causing the tiny, dull invitations of Singlehood—a cultural event and a beer—to sprout.

What I was hoping was that these tough little shrubs (Thai food plus video, Boulez lecture) would blossom into lush forests. Somehow I and the friends I never bothered to call when I *had* a relationship would spontaneously reconnect, staying out until two A.M., laughing, talking, taking up wild new hobbies, starting a small theater troupe, perhaps.

Not so simple. As the newly single person discovers, friends fall into three categories.

1. *Couples.* Good for a few dinners, yes. But by eleven P.M., their eyes glaze over with a look that says, "We made you a meal, we laughed at your jokes, now please leave."

2. *Turbo Singles.* So skilled are they at singing the Songs of Themselves that they will abandon you at museum openings to sing it to someone else . . . someone datable.

3. What one is generally left with, Saturday nights, are the *Depressed Singles:* the suddenly divorced men eager to go out for a drink so you'll get to meet their nine-year-old son, Kevin. Any-

one taking three or more courses at the Learning Annex. Those who keep harping about some woman named Nadia who recently moved to Berlin. "She moved to Berlin!" you want to cry out. "Give it up already!"

All right. What's so bad about staying home by myself—saving money, going to bed early, hauling out recycling as faithfully as a nun? Nothing . . . had I not run afoul of some tofu manicotti. Six boxes worth. That's the problem with Trader Joe—you trust him and suddenly odd tofu things are happening that make you fart. (Vegetable gyoza—don't ask.)

Oh well, each box is only 260 calories—I could have two. The eye of the microwave glared at me. With an ominous buzz, the twin cardboard boxes began their tedious rotation.

As my low-fat/nondairy/no-MSG meal was irradiating, I opened some canned food for the dogs. What were *they* having? Bacon and Cheese Dinner . . . with Gravy! I popped it open to reveal something incredibly moist, tender, pinkish. A heady aroma filled the kitchen. It was the smell of everything marvelous: duck pâté, thin-sliced ham, tuna *in oil* . . .

Lest I lose my head and begin smearing the dog food on toast—selecting a nice wine to go with it—I decided to phone my sister and share all my incredible insights.

"OK, so it's called Trader Joe's," I explained. "But burritos are made by Trader José, manicotti by Trader Giotto, gyozas by Trader Ming. Trader Joe almost becomes a kind of shadowy Big Brother figure, or a schizophrenic. Does he appear sometimes in drag—Trader Joanne?"

"Uh huh," she murmured worriedly. "Listen, being by yourself isn't making you . . . like, *wig out,* is it?"

"No . . . the key to Singlehood, I think, is to fall in love with the image of yourself single," I pressed on, encouraged. "I picture myself staying up alone past midnight in a black cat-suit, listening to Miles Davis's *Kind of Blue,* drinking Glenlivet, reading Céline. Critical, though, is having someone phone me right then to ask what I'm doing. Only then do I get to reveal how self-sufficient I am."

"Mmm," she agrees. But then I hear it. What all Singles dread: the telltale sound of their listener logging onto CompuServe. My "Song of Myself" had become a dirge.

So I've given up. I *am* pathetic—and I'm OK with that. I'll see you next month at the Learning Annex! I've signed up for five classes. I've got some dog food. Bring your son!

Cybersex
Gal

I had cybersex the other night, and, boy, am I sorry.

I didn't mean to have cybersex, of course. I didn't even know I was having it at the time—I just thought my CompuServe mailbox was being jammed with off-color computer mail from a lot of creepy men. I'd clicked the wrong icon in WinCIM by accident, and was trying to wend my way back to . . .

Oh, all right. Let's be frank. It was I, of my own volition, who'd clicked "Access CB Adult II Band."

Because, yes, that's the kind of story this is—a story of incredible squalor and degradation, of me getting grimly naked (sort of) with strangers. If you have a weak stomach, turn the page. Um, also—let me apologize in advance to those of you who know the Mikester (my significant other) and me socially. How terribly awkward. I hope you'll keep inviting us to things. I think we still have your cake pan.

We're fine about the cybersex stuff, by the way. I was worried about what Mike would think, sure. But annoyingly, Mike refuses to fly into a jealous rage—or show even a mild interest. That's the problem, isn't it? People are bored to tears by all this online stuff. It doesn't hold anyone's attention. Which is how I got into trouble in the first place. Let me explain:

I have CompuServe, but use it only to read e-mail. E-mail that's for *me*. (I hate it when people forward me syndicated "Funny Newz": the silliest parking ticket in the world, a boa constrictor pulled out of a toilet, that cow in Biloxi that fell over. Why not just read *Boys Life* magazine and pick my nose?) Problem is, these days no one wants you to use your online service for just that one thing you want—in my case, gossiping peevishly about coworkers. "Know what Sue and Ed paid for their kitchen remodeling?" <send> "No!" <send> "$75,000!" <send> "Why?" <send> "A mistake about sink sizes!" <send>

Completely fulfilled as I am, I've never had any desire to exit e-mail and wander elsewhere in CompuServe to check stock prices, compare airline fares, download video drivers, upload photos of myself with my cat onto the network to show the world how truly alone I feel. Nope, got no curiosity about any of it.

"None?" a friend asked. "Not even about exploring an online adult hot tub?"

I looked up. "An online what?"

"Read the book," he said, whipping out a heavy paperback tome just like they do in those Time-Life commercials. I think his intent was to draw me toward education by dangling the greasy carrot of prurience.

Sadly, the book he gave me about online services was so tedious that I'd skim one paragraph and instantly slump over into a coma.

So I did not actually read the adult hot tubs chapter word for word. Or at all. Instead, I took the idea and ran with it in my own way. Online Hot Tubs! Sophisticated urbanites sharing witty banter as they sip Chardonnay before a rosy Esalen sunset! Kind of a hipster, late-seventies, George Segal/Susan Anspach–type thing! I can go for that, I thought. Swirling my mouse with aplomb, I clicked CB Adult II Band. There was a *Ding!* then an explosion of flying pages, menus, color bars. "Hot . . . tubbin'!" I hooted.

"WHAT IS YOUR HANDLE?" the computer wanted to know.

My handle? At that instant, I swear to God, somewhere in my brain a trapdoor creaked open and out plopped the name "DANIELLE." You know DANIELLE: free-spirited Swedish exchange student, possible herpes sore, into nudity and unicorns.

I don't really want to *be* DANIELLE. On the other hand, if you're going to the trouble of joining an invisible party with invisible people in an invisible hot tub, what's the point of being sensible old JOAN, with her flat-heeled shoes? You know JOAN has only to scoot in next to some oily Santa Cruz lit prof and soon she'll be subsisting on ovo-lacto meals and doing all his typing.

In retrospect, me taking the name DANIELLE was like an iffy skater strapping greased Rollerblades over wobbly ankles and pushing off woodenly down a steep incline. But at the time, what did I know? "Hot . . . tubbin'!" I hooted.

A sentence popped up on my screen: "HI, DANIELLE. IT'S MR. MONTANA. HOW ARE YOU DOING?"

"HEY, MR. MONTANA! I'M DOING GREAT!"

"WOULD YOU LIKE TO COME UP TO MY MOUNTAIN CABIN, DANIELLE?"

See how everyone cuts to the chase when you're European and kind of easy? In real life, I've never, ever been invited to anyone's mountain cabin. I'm a little resentful. And what a cabin this turns out to be: cozy fireplace, shag rugs, massive . . . stereo. MR. MONTANA is all over DANIELLE like a cheap coat.

"I BET YOU'D LIKE A SHOULDER RUB. YOU LOOK HOT TONITE. DO YOU LIKE THE GUITTAR STILINGS OF OTMAR LEEBURT? DO YOU WANT SOME CHAMPAGNE? I HAVE SOME DON PERIONE."

DANIELLE knows she is a wild Swedish exchange student, up for anything, but even she can't ignore the faint odor that hangs in the virtual air—MR. MONTANA is a very bad speller. What will be next—"I WANT TO FONDEL YOUR BRESTESES"?

Just in time, a new suitor pops onto the screen: "HI, DANIELLE, LARRY B. HERE. WHAT ARE YOUR MEASUREMENTS?"

Whereas in three dimensions such a question would draw a sullen look and angry tears, when you're DANIELLE you just laugh and say: "32-22-36! BLONDE, 22! NEW IN THE U.S.! I DRIVE A MIATA!"

LARRY B. is stunned by his luck. "ARE YOU HOME?" he asks.

"NO—WORKING LATE, DOWNTOWN HIGH-RISE, INTERNATIONAL FINANCE. STOCKS, BONDS. TOKYO, BERLIN. NEON, PLEXIGLAS. YOU?"

"I WORK IN SHIPPING AND RECEIVING AT A SMALL AIR CONDITIONER REPAIR COMPANY IN GLENDALE," LARRY B. admits sadly. "I GUESS YOU PROBABLY FIND WHAT I DO PRETTY DULL."

"WOULD YOU LIKE A MASSAGE FROM DR. GOODLOVE?" A new dialogue box has appeared.

"DANIELLE?" springs another. His handle spookily reads "AT THE LAX HYATT." "ARE YOU IN DRIVING DISTANCE? I'M IN RM 227."

Just when the Sleaze-O-Meter overloads, DANIELLE meets SHARON—a warm, funny gal-pal who teaches DANIELLE how to use the "SQUELCH" button and other great tips about WinCIM. They laugh about the horrible men on CB Adult II Band and the absurdity of it all. "IT'S SO NICE TO TALK TO A WOMAN," DANIELLE confides. It is at this point that SHARON tremulously reveals that she is actually a woman trapped in a man's body. She wants DANIELLE'S "help" in "becoming a woman." DANIELLE is unnerved—yet SHARON did give her all those great computer tips. DANIELLE hesitantly suggests that SHARON do estrogen treatments and shave her body hair.

SHARON does. "I'M SHAVING. WHAT KIND OF LOTION DO I USE?"

"WHATEVER YOU LIKE," is the queasy reply.

"OK—AND NOW, WHAT DO YOU WANT ME TO PUT ON?"

DANIELLE wonders if she should suggest kind of a Tim Curry thing. "CORSET, FISHNETS, HEELS."

"OK—NOW, WHAT DO YOU WANT ME TO DO?"

DANIELLE tries to think of the nastiest thing imaginable. Then it comes to her, like a line from an Allman Brothers song: "DANCE FOR ME, HOT MAMA, WITH YOUR PURPLE FEATHER BOA!"

This is not the right thing to say. SHARON hits the SQUELCH button. It is DANIELLE who has become obscene. Let me tell you, nothing makes one feel quite as low as being rejected during cybersex. DANIELLE was crushed. All I can say is, thank God it wasn't me.

Confessions
of the
Dating-Impaired

Memo to every guy I've ever dated:

I'm getting married this month. HA HA HA HA HA HA!!!

My friend Todd (thirty-eight, composer, bachelor) says he may not come: "I hate weddings. They always just symbolize victory for the woman. Then there's the God thing. It really bugs me."

Snipes Steve (thirty-four, lawyer, divorced): "Married? Why? I thought things were going so well."

Then there's Jack (forty-four—but very, very tight stomach, playwright, confirmed bachelor). His flattering new term for me? "The Big Stinky Bride."

With unmined gold like this just sitting out there, it's a wonder I've taken myself out of L.A.'s exciting and fulfilling Dating Scene. But who am I kidding? Let's be honest. (Hey, I can afford to be— I'm the Big Stinky Bride! I'm absolutely swollen with confidence!)

I was never more than a C+ dater anyway. Never did master the basic Dating Skills.

What Dating Skills? Let me think back to the Dark Ages. When I was unattached—a.k.a.: a festering maw of insecurity, Ms. Swamp Thing, so desperate I'd end lonely nights out by leaping with a warbling howl onto the backs of frightened valet parkers.

That's what happens when you carry old DNA into the new system. Emotionally, I'm as complex as our friend the lowly trilobite. I spend one night with a person, the tractor beam locks in, this is my mate for life. Imagine how disastrous. At one point, I was living with (and even weirder, diligently cooking for) a group of rock bagpipe players. (Why? Why?)

What I've learned is, I have terrible judgment. Don't ask me to pick a guy—no, in my case it's "Stop me before I date again." Having the village elders select a goatherd husband actually makes sense for me. I do extremely well in arranged matches. Even in high school, I loved every guy my mother loved. (They'd all grow up to be gay, but how could we know?)

But my Dating ineptitude went beyond the question of choice. Let's say for once I'd be seeing a guy who was perfectly fine. Not a conceptual artist obsessed with things rectal; not a welterweight boxer who bagged groceries at a liquor store; not a Mormon who burst into tears every time he saw my bra. No no no.

This perfect guy would be Phillip. Let us take a moment to contemplate Phillip. You know Phillip, successful magazine writer. He is smart, funny, presentable. Phillip will meet you at Friday MOCA openings with a great haircut and zippy Clacton and Frinton jacket.

(On the other hand, who the hell cares? Nine out of ten times, you'll have much more fun with a person drinking vodka and playing Scrabble in your pajamas. But see how such a reasonable let's-get-to-know-each-other proposal is totally unacceptable as a First Date in today's harsh, cruel, health-crazy Los Angeles.)

Anyhoo, like others of Phillip's ilk—those smart, funny, presentable professional men who form that eerie, hollow-eyed Children of the Corn phalanx across our fair city—the perfect Phillip package was coated with this impenetrable Dating Membrane.

To wit: You were supposed to see Phillip once a week at most, twice a month more typically . . . but you were never to contact him in between. As though he were a kind of undercover spy. To call him at work was to trigger that, that bomb. And of course, post–Women's Lib, said date always included sex. I don't know how we bungled that particular campaign, but we did.

Phillip kept trying, vainly, to train me in the new system. And I knew I should get with it. I knew it was the law of Dating Land. I knew that if I didn't follow it, well, then I would lose my all-important Dating Land citizenship. I wouldn't be allowed to go to the museum twice a month anymore for dull sex with other funny, presentable, hollow-eyed Children of the Corn, etc.

But I just couldn't.

"So-o-o." Phillip would smile suavely in the morning, handing me my delicious fresh-brewed cappuccino mocha symbol-of-a-vast-emptiness-inside (to go). "Call you in ten days?"

"Ten days? That's almost two weeks!" I'd stab out in alarm, eyes wide (picture last night's mascara gone spookily raccoony), vocal pitch a little too high, almost—I'm afraid—*shrieky*.

"I'm Out of Town," he'd enunciate, carefully but firmly, as you do when telling a large-wattled, eager Labrador to "Sit!" but she cannot quite remember how. Phillip repeated the command: "Out of Town. Out of Town. In ten days or so. I will call you."

"Ohhhhh." I'd start to remember the drill. I'd bravely punch him on the arm, give an exaggerated wink to let him know I was "copacetic." Dutifully I recited: "Well, have a great time! Geez, I've got a busy week too! Hey! All right already!" Like those rabbits in that weird warren in *Watership Down*, you never asked Phillip questions that started with "when" or "where."

Know what, though? It's not just women who flail their way across Dating Land. Take my friend Carlos. Tall, handsome, thirty-three, articulate, hilarious, brilliant composer (L.A. Philharmonic commissions, rave reviews in the *Times*—it's all in place).

The problem? I won't sugar-coat it for you, ladies. Like me, Carlos has the old DNA. His is the model that came out before the Teflon-coated T-2000. He is the Dating-impaired.

Here's roughly how it goes. Carlos meets a woman at a party; she likes him. He gets the number, makes the call, sets up the Friday Date. Everyone is happy. But then he does what I call "The Carlos Fumble." He calls later the same day to try for a Sunday Matinee Date as well. That's in addition to the Friday Date. Mysteriously, the woman starts cancelling, becoming "very busy," not calling back (and of course, the No Call is a Call).

"You can't do this!" I protest. "To call twice in the same day— to set up two weekend dates at once? Before you've even had the first date? To today's busy professional woman, you seem desperate and sad."

But Carlos never gets it.

"If I'm interested, I'm interested," he says plaintively. "I want to get to know the woman better. What are we waiting for?" You can almost hear the flap of pterodactyls overhead.

Finally, I have to sympathize. After all, Carlos is one of my people. Skillful Daters juggle other Daters with ease; their voices never crack with need; they're experts at noncommitment. The rest of us lurch around like Quasimodo, an embarrassment to society, continually botching the Dating ballet. We suck at Dating because for us, it's about rules of distance; it's the opposite of passion; it's the very talisman of noninterest.

Thank God I've given it all up and graduated to Big Fat Wedding Cow. In the meantime, if there are any girls out there with the old, defective DNA, call me. I'll set you up with a gem of a guy. As for the rest of you: Hey, I'll call you sometime! Really.

How
to Talk
Dirty

Granted, there are folks for whom dirty talk seems to come easily: men with receding hairlines and gold chains at singles' bars; construction workers; Clarence Thomas. From past sexual exploits to unprovable estimates of one's own penis size, no topic goes untouched.

Nor is this talent confined to men. Females who've talked a blue streak, I've been told, have included Salt Lake City cocktail waitresses; six-foot-tall Texas divorcées on their way to L.A. but "laying over" in Denver; and twenty-two-year-old New York art dealer assistants named Amanda with slight coke problems.

Whichever way you slice the pie, 80 percent of the world remains. Most of us are interested in dirty talk, yes we are—but we hesitate. We see talking dirty as a kind of leap across the abyss. If you make it, well, you've just saved yourself a lot of time, and had some chuckles in the process. If you don't, you plummet to a humiliating death. No wonder most of us shake our heads, saddle up our burros, and quietly go the long way round.

Even shy people should take the plunge more often, though, because the rules that govern effective dirty talk are not that complicated.

Briefly, dirty talk tends to excite us when:

1. It comes from a person we actually find attractive, as opposed to some random mat-haired individual on the subway.
2. The timing is good.
3. It's believable. For some reason, people find "I'm going to _____ you 'til you sweat" more exciting than "I'm going to _____ you 'til you explode." Who knows why.
4. The exact words used are vulgar enough to make our pubic hair stand on end, but not so vulgar they cause us to giggle at, slap, or even sue the person.

The actual lexicon to be worked from is simplicity itself. "Fuck me," "suck me," "tits," "cock," all told, there are about twelve basic words that work 90 percent of the time. It's amazing how undiverse America is in that one particular way: it's Pavlovian. There's rarely any need to get fancy. In fact, the more the speaker deviates from the handbook, the less we tend to like it.

Consider, for instance, that as an appellation for the male member, nothing really beats "cock." "Dick" seems to lack the same punch, "rod" can be iffy (really depends on the neighborhood). From there you go on to terms like "willy," "bone," "schlongeroo," and even cutesy nicknames like "Mr. Friendly" (i.e., "How is Mr. Friendly feeling this morning?").

Such mock endearments might be fine for a moment's amusement, yes, but do they really make us feel nasty? Perhaps the most loathsome penile nomer I've heard is "stem"—as in, "You want a little stem?" I don't know why. It's just awful. Better to stick with words you hear on standard-issue porn videos (avoid the sub-titled ones).

Beyond this, we begin to move into the murky realm of gender differences. Males, overall, tend to be more forgiving of such sub-tleties as word choice, rhythm, inflection, etc.

My friend Jeff, for instance, is open to dirty talk of any kind, any kind at all. Basically, he appreciates whatever show of enthu-siasm his partner can muster; the words "yes, yes"—heck, even a simple "okay"—are enough to get him going, "Dirty talk is good; clean talk is good—geez." He sighs. "The fact that I'm *having sex at all* is good! If she's talking, maybe this means she'll want to do it again some time. That's pretty cool."

Steven has a more discerning ear. "Sometimes women can go too far. This one girl and I met in a bar, went home to her apart-ment. She had this huge four-poster bed, huge pillows. In the middle of everything, she starts saying things like: 'Ride me, cow-boy!' and 'Ow! Ow! You're so big, I can't take it! Ow! Ow! Ride me!' I kind of went, 'Huh?' It really turned me off. I was too big for her? I knew this couldn't possibly be true."

In fact, sex therapists have long understood that it's better to say to a man "You're so hard" than "You're so big." The big men will think "big" is what you *really* meant to say, while the less well-endowed will . . . well, they'll think they're really hard.

Other mild turn-offs cited include women who talk all the way through, and women who continually issue commands.

And we're not talking dominatrix-style commands; we're talking commands spoken in that certain tone of voice, full of accusations and laundry and dishes, that can render the sexual experience absolutely nullifying: "Lick me there—no there. Harder! Softer! All right. I'm ready. Give me your cock. Hurry." At such times, the female orgasm seems to hover as tiny and elusive as Luke Skywalker's target on the Death Star.

Abused in this way, dirty words will cease to become dirty talk at all. A woman's flat command, "Eat me," will actually become depressing—particularly when you know, from past experience, that this is an arduous procedure that will take forty minutes, culminating most probably in tears and an argument. Much better form, always, is for the woman to lustily cry out "Eat me!" when her partner is already doing so, and quite well indeed. See? That small shift in timing makes it dirty.

As far as their tastes and distastes go, women are all over the board. My friend Nancy wants you to say her name during sex: "Nancy, Nancy, oh, Nancy." That is, if she likes you. If she doesn't, she'd prefer you forgot her name entirely.

Lynn admits a weakness for statements like: "Oh, baby, you taste so good." She explains, "It's nice to be told that my bodily secretions are delightful rather than disgusting. That tends to boost confidence." Turn-offs include over-fixation on the male member, as in: "Oh, baby, my cock is this, my cock is that, don't you want my cock? Hey! Look over here! There it is again: my cock." Weirdly enough, the woman hears this and instantly assumes the speaker has a lot of trouble holding erections.

Most crucial to note, finally, are areas where men and women turn heel and head in opposite directions completely.

Men like forceful statements of intention—that enthusiasm thing again. A husky "I want to suck your cock" or "I'm going to suck your cock" is preferable to the more pallid "Would you like me to suck your cock?" In fact a woman can never go wrong with the basic sentence structure: "I'm going to ____ you 'til you moan," as long as the blank refers to any sexual act, not to a relationship discussion.

Women, on the other hand, are much more picky. Announcements like "I'm going to enter you anally now" can easily go awry. Note how the appropriate negotiations need to be made well, *well* beforehand. On the other hand, during foreplay, some breathy remark along the lines of "I'd really, *really* like to fuck you now. Oh, could I, *could* I?" might well work, implying that she is the queen and that he is her slave boy, a scenario that seems to work nicely for everybody.

Too, men are generally amused at being called things in bed, probably because typical male sexual appellations have a sort of cheerful outdoorsy quality. "Cowboy," "sailor," and "stud" come to mind. The thought that it could be their photo on the wrapper for Brawny paper towels puts men in a jolly mood. On the other hand, addressing one's female partner by such names as "bitch" or "whore" soon becomes very dismal and *Taxi Driver*.

Then again, if it's all too exhausting, you can forget the whole dirty-talk issue and just moan a lot. Works for me.

Lesbian
Pool Party

You can almost hear "Holiday for Strings" as we swing into the circular drive of the three-star Palm Springs Riviera Resort. "Riviera!" proclaims the pink-and-white logo in the flowing curves of a signature scrawled in lipstick. Sheathed in Mediterranean white, flanked with palms, dotted with flowers, the Riviera has that posh Ricardo Montalban-esque feel so native to Palm Springs.

Like most of the women here this sunny March weekend, my friend Jess and I have come, ostensibly, for the Dinah Shore Golf Tournament. But it's the ancillary events that really excite us. Like the ones in the Riviera package produced by Club Skirts/Girl Bar; from the "Riv," they tell us, you can walk to Friday's "Le Moulin Rouge" ("with 3,000 *très chic* women"), Saturday's "Monte Carlo Madness" ("4,000 Women"), and Sunday's "French Riviera Pool Party" ("featuring the Jägermeister Poster Models"). We'll miss Klub Banshee's "Outrageous Women in Uniform Party," though. So many babes, so little time.

Two by two, women are arriving: by Harley, by van, by Mustang convertible, by neat gray Honda Accord. We lug tennis rackets, garment bags, purses and keys, things Nike, things Gucci, and cash for our fees. And Visa. You have to. For Party Passports, which get you into "Le Moulin Rouge," "Monte Carlo Madness," and the pool party: forty dollars. *Ka-ching*. For tonight's "Funny Girlz" comedy show and dance party: thirty dollars. Golf day passes: fifteen dollars. *Ka-ching, ka-ching*. Saturday's "Desert Palms Bra Party," to which "partygoers are invited to wear their sexiest and most unusual bras," is free.

Small point one: I have brought only lousy bras. My job is to cover the scene, not create it. Small point two: Back in L.A., my journalistic "date" Jess and I live with men. But then we are handed our tokens de resort—minibar key and pool passes. "What the hell?" we think. "The cocktails are frosty and the bodies are hot! We're red-blooded gals! We can at least *look*, can't we? Let's get crazy"—*clink*—"in Palm Springs!"

What straight woman hasn't had a lesbian fantasy? I certainly have. My own Sapphic holiday takes place on some glittering remote island in the Caribbean populated by the likes of Brigitte Nielsen, Theresa Russell, and Jacqueline Bisset.

Stretched out gloriously under the palms like a jungle cat, in orange bikini top and sarong, Jacqueline Bisset flashes a sidelong glance from under her sun hat. She is growing tired of her book (*Taipan*, by James Clavell) and has drained three whiskey sours. "Oh, *hell!*" she hisses, mouth slack, scanning the beach in vain for Raphael the houseboy, who has her cigarettes.

Under the umbrella of such glamorous boredom, It happens. Understand that I have no idea what I myself am wearing or what I say or anything. I am a disembodied Emersonian eye that floats over everything. Over everything James Bond: the Caribbean, cocktails, sloshed Eurotrash models with lax morals. . . .

None of which has anything to do with actual lesbian life. Or so I've always thought.

Ten years ago my college roommate Martha was drifting into a new phase. She'd cropped off her hair, was volunteering ten hours a week at the Rape Hotline, began working with the women's soccer team, bought Holly Near records, played pool with older, heavyset women at Vermies in Pasadena. All fine and good.

Then one Friday night I strode into our apartment, boyfriend in tow. Martha and a dozen of her crop-haired, soccer-playing girlfriends lay on sleeping bags in the living room, talking and laughing, beer bottles and chips around them. When I poked my head in to say a cheery hello: dead silence.

OK, maybe I was straight. But I had that Jackie Bisset fantasy—there couldn't be that huge an abyss between us. Then I furtively paged through Martha's *Joy of Lesbian Sex*.

Never in my wildest dreams had I envisioned *this*. These were not erotic, *Penthouse*-y photos but pencil illustrations of a grimly realistic, doggedly multicultural sort. Women of color, women of thighs, women of imperfect skin, women of wrinkled lumberjack shirts and no panties. Nary a deftly done silicone job was to be seen. They pushed coffee tables aside and grappled each other with large, cellulite-mottled gams.

In short, these women looked exactly like me. Where was the

Christie Brinkley fantasy pullout? When I came to a chapter entitled "Yeast Infections," I had to put it down.

But this was the early eighties. We're talking Jurassic history. In that era, Martina Navratilova was just another terrific tennis player. k. d. lang was shopping demo tapes. Madonna was still a boy toy. Whitney Houston wasn't married to Bobby Brown.

Today, anyone who thinks lesbians can't be sexy, glamorous—not to mention politically incorrect—has obviously not been to Palm Springs's Dinah Shore Golf Weekend, also known as the "largest dyke party west of the Mississippi."

The weekend was established in 1972, when Colgate-Palmolive Co. initiated the Dinah Shore Golf Tournament, which has since become a major stop on the LPGA circuit. (Nabisco took over corporate sponsorship in 1982.) A combination of elements—the fact that some lesbians like golf, that the weather in Palm Springs is always terrific in March—made the Dinah Shore a convenient annual meeting place. Since then, the face of the weekend has changed radically. In the early seventies, lesbians were trying to scrape together clusters of twenty-five to book Palm Springs hotels. Today, the whole town is overrun, a magnet for diverse groups. There are the older, more closeted lesbians; the twenty-ish "girl bar" crowd; the professionals; the golfing diehards. The mix is intercultural, intergenerational.

Yes, the five thousand or so Dinah Shore lesbians stay at different hotels (ranging from swanky to cheesy, depending on one's funds), move with different cliques, and enjoy their own often mutually exclusive forms of entertainment. There are discreet doctors and lawyers who wouldn't be caught dead watching whipped cream wrestling night at Daddy Warbucks. But one thing unites: All enjoy the group energy—and all are ready to party and spend. Crisp hundred-dollar bills flutter across cash bars. The luxurious, 480-room Riviera Resort alone finds itself 90 percent lesbian-booked for the weekend.

Do the math and you'll understand why the Palm Springs Chamber of Commerce is finding itself increasingly upbeat about alternative lifestyles. As Robin Tyler, a lesbian comic and producer, puts it: "What's reflected in Dinah Shore is an international, global movement. Our space has moved from bars to festivals to cruises to international travel. Lesbian life has changed from movement to industry. Traditional business finally sees us as a market. After all, the average annual income of a gay household is $42,000, lesbian $36,000. Compared with the average American household's $30,000, we have a lot of disposable income!"

So while the nineties may be tough for most, the decade is becoming a boom time for lesbians. No wonder there's hedonism in the air. Forget the social-justice agenda—Dinah Shore lesbians are here to party. The once de rigueur ducktail haircuts and tweed jackets are a thing of the past. Now all costumes are permitted: strawberry lip gloss, nail polish, heels. Think Lesbian Spring Break at Fort Lauderdale. Think mondo pool parties, string bikinis, and beyond. Think Girls' Summer Camp Gone Hog Wild—and *without* Tom Selleck there to play athletic director.

The red message light is flashing when we get to our room. It's from our informal Dinah Shore "guide," Leah.

I've arranged in advance for a kind of Sapphic sherpa/guide/
protector for the weekend. I thought a friendly lesbian might
come in handy if Jess and I were to find ourselves at some
"Desert Bra Party" swung out of control. ("Strip and get into the
conga line!" I envision some woman resembling Billie Jean King
on an off-day commanding us. "Or are you . . . *straight*?")

Leah, twenty-six, is a co-worker's sister's friend. Well, not exactly "friend." You have to understand the complicated nuances
of lesbian relationships. In truth, three years ago, Leah had an af-
fair with the sister. Even though Leah was still living with Ann.
Who I know from a writer's group. Who soon left Leah to move
in with her karate instructor, Tracie. Word has it Ann has since
split from Tracie and is now secretly doing it with Karen, who is
living with Leah. To further muddy the waters, all still work out at
the dojo owned by Tracie and her new lover, Beth, who can break
bricks with her hands.

On the phone, Leah's news is not good. She isn't in Palm
Springs yet, she says. She and Karen had a fight and didn't leave
Laguna until late. (Karen is a freelance graphic artist, while
Leah—in perfect dyke blue-collar chic—is a mail carrier.) But
Leah says she'll be sure to find us tonight at "Le Moulin Rouge."
Among "3,000 *très chic* women." Right.

Deflated as Jess and I are, our moods rise after we shower—
separately—and change. We then hit town for the show.

The Palm Springs evening is glittering and balmy. Magically,
the city has been transformed into Planet of the Women. In parking lots, sidewalks, lobbies—everywhere—there are girls: girls
from Dallas, girls from Seattle, girls from San Diego; old girls,
young girls, fat girls, tan girls, biker girls, jeans girls, girls with

dual Conway Twitty haircuts, groping girls, drinking girls, laughing girls, girls standing together in fierce silence.

"I can't *believe* you gave Lisa those tickets!" one buffed-out blonde in a visor screams at her partner. "That's fifty dollars!"

There's PMS lurking around the edges. "I STILL LOVE MARTINA!" screams the cover of *Lesbian News;* so says Texas beauty and former Navratilova lover, Judy Nelson. "'I was her wife,'" we read. "'She wanted one, she got one, and I was the best damned one she ever had.'"

But tonight, you can't help feeling all the snits will be forgotten, all sisters united. Like a pulse, an energy, good vibes grow among the several thousand women at the Palm Springs Convention Center. The "Funny Girlz" event stand-up routines are hilarious. Even Jess and I catch on to the Whitney Houston jokes, the Long Beach Federal Express women jokes, and why lesbians are horrified to find new lovers wearing Lee Press-On nails.

Afterward, jostling out with the crowd, a group elation is palpable. Pooh-pooh the communal power of wymmenfolk if you will: females love being together. The sheer safety of it buoys confidence. Usually my 125-pound girlfriend and I are a target when we're out alone at night. Now it's a pleasure. After all, Jess—slim, mascara-ed, cool hair—is my "trophy" date. You have to be an idiot not to notice. I must be *pretty hot* to be with her!

Woop! Someone squeezes my butt! Gaily, I whip around and squeeze her back. I hope it's the right person. Who cares? We're all equals! I can be butt-squeezer one moment and butt-squeezee the next. I don't have to cringe in a corner, clutching my purse. I can be the pervert in the trenchcoat if I choose! I can feel a tit, grab a crotch, wolf-whistle!

The heat turns up at "Le Moulin Rouge" at Bono's nightclub. Downstairs, R&B star Sabrina Johnston is performing her hit(?), "Peace in the Valley." One gal, in unbuttoned jacket and bra, leaps onto the stage, gyrating and shimmying for the mob. "Woo! You *go,* girl!" we all shriek. It's utterly natural, even for straight women. (Don't forget that one of our curious customs is the lingerie party—females wearing sexy lingerie and parading around for each other.) We twist to the disco beat, sweat breaking out on our foreheads. Show, show, show! Dance, dance, dance!

"Sandra?"

I turn around.

"Oh, my God!"

Can it be . . . my old college roommate, *Martha*? But yes, there she stands, looking much the same as she did back in her soccer days—short hair, white blouse, bike pants. A lithe, similarly clad brunette hangs on to her arm.

"What are *you* doing here?" she crows.

"What are *you*?" I counter.

As a matter of fact, it is Martha and Felice's second visit to Dinah Shore. They use it as their annual break, Felice being busy with vet school, Martha with her thriving career in computer marketing. Unlike younger counterparts such as Leah and Karen, they are solid professionals. They live in Albuquerque, where they own a house. "We come to Dinah Shore to ogle," Martha explains, relaxed and humorous in her thirties. "It's a kick. They sure don't have anything like this at home."

Jess and I are only too glad to connect with trusty Martha. Be-

cause the red message-light is flashing again the next morning—
Leah's latest update. Leah says she *did* manage to drag Karen into
town last night, but too late for Bono's. Now, she says, Karen's
gone shopping for a few hours while she's going to crash.

She'll be "sure" to find us later at the golf tournament.

In fact, most of our Riviera cohorts show little interest in golf
this sunny Saturday morning. Many loll about the pool; a few are
busier. Opposite our room, a sand volleyball court stands right
next to an asphalt basketball court. To the volleyball side gravitate
the blond Southern California beach-goddess lesbians. To the
basketball side go lesbians of color with brutal duck-tail haircuts,
in hightop street gear. "Come on, girl," they scream. "*Move* the
ball! *Move* the ball!"

Nothing, however, compares with the golf. The beautiful Palm
Springs day, the whispering trees, the rolling lawns . . .

There are the apple-shaped women in pageboy haircuts,
sports visors, Polo shirts, and Bermudas striding across the man-
icured green, the cringing male caddies and the hushed audiences
tiptoeing after them. Here achievement is discussed in "holes,"
not in bats or balls. When the tiny ball drops into the waiting Hole,
the crowd calls out, "Ahhh!" after one sharp intake of breath.

Poor Dinah Shore. She just happens to love golf—and spon-
sors love her. As she told *Desert Golf* magazine: "Golf is like a
lousy lover. It's like some guy who is never there when you need
him. I have fallen deeply in love with this game. I get a headache
if I can't get a game. And I will get this game if it kills me."

Does she know how many lesbians hold her banner aloft?

. . .

"I really want to wear my cute pin, but what if it falls off in the crowd? Who will care anyway. I'm not anyone's *type*."

"Thin pants or flowery skirt? Which is more lesbian?" Jess grouses. "I haven't had my butt pinched *once*."

Having gotten just four hours of sleep the night before, we thirtyish types are tired and irritable. And here we are getting dressed for our second (sigh) wild evening of partying.

We needn't have worried about our looks. "Monte Carlo Madness," in the Riviera's le Grande Ballroom, is so big, dark, and noisy no one notices us at all. It is a sci-fi warehouse: lasers cut through the air; technofunk blasts across the ballroom; three go-go dancers gyrate in cages high in the air. Oglers can have their choice: James Bond gal with hair flip and bell-bottoms, tomboy in coveralls, blonde leatherette in black push-up bra and hot pants. We are literally stunned into passivity by the spectacle.

Tonight's mood, too, is different. Whereas Friday's was euphoric, Saturday's has an edgy, "last night of the convention" feel. If you're going to get laid, it has to happen tonight.

If I were looking, I find myself wondering, whom would I want?

Would I want a girl-as-boy? Dancing in one corner is a person who looks exactly like a guy I'd had a crush on in high school: slim hips, longish hair, John Lennon sunglasses. That androgynous beatnik look is a turn-on in a way trying-too-hard "macho" duck-tail haircuts aren't. And unlike that guy in high school, this "fellow" wouldn't reject me. How could he? He doesn't have a penis! After all, I've been spurned in my life by a hundred men, but never a woman. Women are my friends, allies. . . .

Would I want a girl-as-sexpot? Jess and I find ourselves mesmerized under the go-go cage of the blonde leatherette nympho. She has terrific tits and an aerobically tight butt, which she bumps and grinds with a cool professional acumen. And yet, staring up her crack, I don't feel aroused. I feel depressed. Jess puts it succinctly: "If I did StairMaster an hour a day, my butt would never look like that."

Aye, that's the rub. That was the beauty of my Jackie Bisset/ *Sports Illustrated* Swimsuit Edition fantasy. How convenient to have been an invisible Emersonian eye. Jackie could never look up at me, scowling, and say: "Sandra? I know *I* look fabulous, but how 'bout you? Those inner thighs are disgusting!"

The crowd parts, and there, at the eleventh hour, stands Leah in lipstick lesbian glory—mini, eyeshadow, heels. Can it be a mirage? "Leah! You made it! Where's Karen?"

"Karen's on her way," Leah says curtly, and turns to me. "You wanna dance? C'mon." She pulls me roughly along, body pressed to mine.

What's happening? My heart is pounding. Where are we going with this? All I know is that I'm finally dancing with a lesbian, an actual lesbian! (It was clearly the right move to go with the cute pin.) I move my hips to the music. I do my best shimmy. Under slitted eyes, I glance at Leah.

Only to realize that Leah is looking at everything but me. We are moving together, yes, but over my shoulder she surreptitiously scans the crowd. Then it dawns on me. She is setting up another scene. I am a prop. Karen comes, finds her already dancing, throws drink in face.

Great, I think. I've come to Palm Springs and abandoned my

best friend to be rejected by a lesbian who isn't even my type! For this I got *dressed up*!

The red message-light is not blinking Sunday morning.

"I'm ready to return to the real world." Jess sighs. Moving slowly, we pack our bags, drink our coffee, brush our teeth.

We say our good-byes to Martha and Felice in the lobby. Out of all of us, they seem the most balanced. "I'm sorry we never got to meet your friend Leah," Martha says.

"Leah who?" Felice leans forward. Then she chuckles. "Oh . . . I think I know her. *From Tracie's dojo?*"

"That dojo must really be something," Jess says. "Remind me never to study karate."

"As for me," I admit, "I guess I'll just stick with men. It's easier. We've been talking about getting married soon."

"Oh, God, I'd love to get married!" Felice exclaims. We all look at her in horror.

"No, really! I'd love to have a June wedding. The dresses, the showers, the dishes. I love all that corny stuff. It's impossible with my family. They still tell everyone Martha and I are roommates. After seven years."

Martha waits a beat before her quick, "You ready for the drive back?"

On our way out, Jess and I take one more look back at the fabulous Planet Lesbos that is Dinah Shore. It's not my Jackie Bisset Caribbean island, but when I squint my eyes it could be.

The bright Palm Springs sun, bobbing blue water, hundreds of bikini-clad women chatting, sunning, drinking. Jägermeister poster models strutting their stuff. Topless women of size French-kissing in a deck chair. A lesbian rock 'n' roll band banging out covers while a Stevie Nicks type stands to the right, signing for the deaf. "I'm going to leave you, you bitch!" she signs deftly. Then comes a love ballad: "I—just—want—to—go—down—on—you!"

"Stevie" makes a V with her fingers and flicks her tongue through them. The crowd screams, rapt in these last few moments of endless summer.

Tonya Harding, Actress

Memo to Hollywood: Yes, Tonya Harding can act.

Granted, not everyone will care. Industry opinion has long been against the plucky skater from Oregon. Even through-the-roof name recognition and a mean triple-axel couldn't land her a spot in the post-Olympic "Ice Capades" tour. "Saturday Night Live" tapped rival Nancy Kerrigan, not Harding. That way too went the A-list endorsements: Revlon, Disney, and Campbell's soup.

Harding may yet have a future beyond Lillehammer, and beyond the probation she now serves for knowing a little too much about Kerrigan's clubbing a little too early. Last weekend she received permission to leave Oregon for several days to make her acting debut in the low-budget action film *Breakaway*. Produced by Breakaway Productions, the film, which is due out late this year, is about a female courier who wants to break away (get it?) from the Mafia. Harding plays "a feisty waitress" who finds $1 million of mob money and runs off to Tahiti.

"I had no expectations about Tonya's performance," admitted thirty-two-year-old *Breakaway* director, co-producer, and co-writer Sean Dash. "We figured this was a no-lose situation."

As it turns out, Harding's participation was a fluke. Living in Portland, far from the firm hands of CAA and PMK, Harding must field film offers on gut instinct. *Breakaway*, being executive produced by Century Film Partners (whose other movies include *Texas Payback* and *Fists of Iron*), was the first one that felt right. Co-producer Eric Gardner, from Harding's hometown, managed to convince her that it would be a fun, low-risk project with a supportive crew.

"Protection" is Gardner's watchword when it comes to handling Harding. "Protection. No one will bother her."

"Tonya is here to shoot a movie. Not to answer any questions. Not to talk to the press" is how Harding's new boyfriend, Doug Lemon, put it, an enigma in a crewcut and wraparound sunglasses, arms folded across his chest.

No wonder members of the press approach the aspiring starlet gingerly: "I hate the *L.A. Times,*" the skater told associate producer Michael Muller in turning down a request for an interview. "They wrote something bad about me once." "I don't think Tonya is making the distinction right now between Sports and Calendar," Muller says.

A reporter from *USA Today*, an old friend of Dash's and therefore on the inside track, did not even try for a direct quote. "I'm just hanging out," he said, hands up. *Entertainment Tonight*, however, fared worst of all. It was banned from the set entirely and forced to sit on the street, cameras and all.

Public relations, however, proves to be the only bobble of the weekend. Within the *Breakaway* family, cast and crew are as one. Excess tensions are handled in the way of the film's celebrity guest—quaffing Mountain Dews and chain-smoking Marlboro Lights. At one point, a production assistant weaves through the group distributing whole packs.

On the set, Harding's behavior is model perfect. She submits easily to a make-over. Stepping onto the set, Gina the Feisty Waitress bears scant likeness to the red-sequined spitfire that riveted Lillehammer. Gone is the temple-winching ponytail; in its place is softly loose blonde hair. Natural-looking makeup brings out electric blue eyes. A modest blue dress flutters.

"You're much prettier than I expected!" exclaims Century Film Partners co-founder Aron Schiffman, shaking her hand.

Harding is also extremely disciplined. She repeats lines and blocks take after take. She even ad-libs good dialogue when necessary. When lines referring to a gun are cut, a new question is put to her character: "Do you know how to fight?" "I can take care of myself," she snaps, not missing a beat.

As such, she draws unanimous raves from her co-stars. Since *Breakaway*'s budget is slightly less than the $1 million Gina the Feisty Waitress discovers in her fridge, the cast does not include big names such as Charlie Sheen or Emilio Estevez. Their uncle, actor Joe Estevez, however, has proved available.

Estevez resembles a burlier version of brother Martin Sheen. His acting has that husky, faintly hammy quality popular in the action genre. In fact, while Estevez may be less known to the public than other family members, he may well have acted in more films. Just a few include *Body Count, The Summoned, Crim-*

inal Intent, The Flesh Merchant, and *Double Blast* (with Linda Blair).

The veteran actor, who has the task of partnering Harding in her very first on-camera scenes, likes what he sees.

"Instinct, that's what Tonya has. Instinct," Estevez says. "She's a nice little actor. It's like Robert Mitchum said, 'Learning acting is like learning to grow tall. Either you do or you don't.' Tonya has the raw talent.

"I think she could do rather well in films. She's got a really great look, she's got a fantastic body, she's very photogenic. People forget that she's just a baby. She must have a lot of discipline and determination to do the things she's done in life, you know? So movies—why not? Why the hell not?"

"If she wants to, she could move right up to big action parts," agrees second unit director Cole McKay. He supervised Harding's first fight scene, which required her to throw a punch at a bad guy, kick him twice, and then hurl him down some stairs. "Here's a woman who's an athlete, who knows how to choreograph moves in her head. She'd make suggestions too, things like, 'I punch better with my right hand than with my left.'"

Would *Breakaway*'s crew work with Harding again?

"Absolutely," enthusiastically confirms director Dash. "I've had less trouble with her than with many other actresses."

Such a positive buzz comes as no surprise to the self-described "brave people" who believed from the start Harding could turn things around. "She can do more than just skate," declares her current manager, Portland-based Merrill Eichenberger, who says his client has been offered roles on Fox-TV's "Married . . . With

Children" and CBS's upcoming comedy series "SHE TV." Eichenberger has an extensive background in marketing and video, describing himself as "one of the pioneers of the infomercial."

"I took Mickey Rooney's career out of the ashcan in 1971—we can do the same for Tonya," agrees Ruth Webb, the partner of Harding's talent agent, Sherri Spillane.

"Look at Vanessa Williams—eight years later, she's opening on Broadway," points out Spillane. "Of course, we're hoping it won't take eight years!"

Faces
International

Who knows what incites adults who've never bothered to audition for even their high school production of *The Diary of Anne Frank* to get up one morning and say, "To hell with a real-estate license. I want to act"? Immortality? Money? The thought of Oscar bookends? Getting a nail wrap without an appointment?

But in L.A. you hear it all the time, and not just from the entertainment subworld of waiters, stylists, production assistants, Holiday Health Spa attendants. The acting bug is grabbing real people, the kind with health insurance who live in Inglewood or Glendale, even Long Beach: truck drivers, medical technicians, airport controllers, mortgage bankers.

They are getting photos "done"; exclaiming "Mm! Maaa!" (warm up those vocal cords) every morning before the mirror; making pilgrimages to Samuel French Bookshop to purchase *Respect for Acting* by Uta Hagen. Suffice it to say, about six thousand of them a year accept a certain open invitation from Faces International to embark on the most glamorous quest in the world. How mellifluous seem the opening cadences of the Faces International TV spot. And I dimly recall the company's Sunset Boulevard billboard bearing the faces of four winsome, if totally unfamiliar, people. Shots of models and actresses in exotic locales while magical words are spoken:

"Have you ever dreamed of pursuing an exciting career in modeling and acting?"

What the hell: I'm sick of my job. I want a Lear jet. I want a more exciting career. I want to, too.

Faces International of Los Angeles, California, can provide the exposure essential for "breaking into the areas of acting, modeling, print work, or commercials." Faces International has helped "hundreds of people" just like me, primarily through a glossy quarterly publication that is distributed internationally (thirty-two countries) to some thirteen thousand of the top casting directors, producers, and agents in "the Industry" (in Faces literature the "I" tends to be capitalized).

The question is, "Am I marketable?"

Interested parties are invited to call 47-FACES to make an appointment for a free one-hour evaluation.

I dial. "Thank you for calling Faces International" (emphasis on "International").

The British accent on the machine is real. It's that of a cool model-turned-administrator, the kind who is likely to ask, "Can you hold? I have Paris on line two." Visions arise of all kinds of slim-hipped seventeen-year-old French girls breezing in and out, carelessly banging huge Helmut Newton–shot portfolios against their impossibly coltish legs. I'm seized with panic. Am I doing something stupid? I'm not seventeen, not particularly slim-hipped, and cursed by sadly little "on camera" experience.

And yet the talent counselor who finally picks up makes it so easy for me. He does not scream, "Are you kidding? You?" when I confess my desire to come to Faces International for my free talent evaluation. "We'll see you tomorrow at 6:30," he says, making a note of it. And then he adds portentously, "Good luck."

OFFICE USE ONLY

Attitude ☐ Photogenic ☐ Personality ☐ Availability ☐
Commitment ☐ Talent ☐ Tenacity ☐

I sit, with a handful of other applicants, mostly in their twenties, in the waiting room at the Century City headquarters of Faces International. We all try to look cool, as though we don't care, as though we already have agents. Phones ring; talent counselors in strange yet chic outfits, clipboards clutched to their chests, hurry in and out of the central offices.

From a video monitor on one side of the room, tanned, gregarious Faces International president George Goldberg talks to us hopefuls about the tools we will need to make it in this business.

Do we need talent? Do we need looks? Would we be better off sleeping with Aaron Spelling?

Nah. While these advantages may be helpful, Goldberg's emphatic message for fledgling actors and models—his Dianetics of TV spokesmodel-hood—concerns a whole level of being, beyond. If he, George Goldberg, were asked (and apparently he is asked quite often: gold-framed photos on the walls show him locked in a death embrace with such industry figureheads as Diahann Carroll, George Burns, Tony Danza, and Michael Landon), "George, what would you say is the one thing a person needs to get started in the entertainment field?" he would unhesitatingly answer, "An unwavering commitment."

Successful actors have described this to him as a kind of "inner urge" to be in front of the camera. The prospective applicant should examine himself or herself: "Do I have this inner urge?" If the answer is no, or even maybe, Goldberg advises, "Go ahead and become a computer operator or a civil-service worker."

Deeply troubled, I turn to the Faces International pre-evaluation questionnaire:

—How long have I been interested in the entertainment industry?
—What motivated me to do something about it now?
—Do I personally know anyone in the industry?
—Am I prepared to do something about a new career now?
—Do I go after what I want, or do I wait for it to come to me?

Scenes from *Death of a Salesman* flash before me. I see myself sitting at the last computer terminal, the one at the very back of data processing, at the DeVry Institute of Technology, waiting, waiting as the enormous parade of life passes me by and all that is left is the limp sac of a popped balloon.

I'm grateful for end questions such as "Which three radio stations do you listen to the most?"

At least I know the answer.

. . .

She's Downtown Julie Brown in the body of Ursula Andress. Talent counselor Brida and I are having a tête-à-tête. It is Brida who will be administering my evaluation. She attempts to set me at ease with some show-biz chat.

"When I first came here from England," Brida recalls, "I could find absolutely no work. I had done runway all over Europe; I had my tearsheets with me—everything. And then I discovered commercials. Great pay, and you can go ahead and weigh 120 if you want to." I turn white. She breezes right on, handing me a copy of *Faces International, the Spring Book*.

"Did you see *The Golden Child*?" she asks, as I flip through the tome. Hundreds of faces gaze out at me. Fat faces. Thin faces. Black faces. White faces. Three-year-old faces. Sixty-year-old faces. Faces flexing mini-barbells; faces chatting on the phone; faces swinging tennis rackets; faces mugging hilariously over burnt pots; faces playing electric guitar; faces stepping out of Alfa Romeos.

"What?"

"*The Golden Child*. Eddie Murphy Productions. Do you know that the baby boy in that film was discovered through Faces International? Yup. Funny thing is, it was a girl. They shaved her head." Brida mugs hilariously. "Got $2 million."

"Two million?"

Brida clucks her tongue. "For $2 million I'd shave my head. I'll tell you that much!"

The moment of truth has come. I am asked to do my first cold reading ever.

I perform a commercial for Visa Gold—a short, first-person tale about having one's car break down in the snow and Whoops! No cash!—at perhaps one of the highest pitches of hysteria I have ever experienced. The text is only about six lines long, but I'm hyperventilating. I hope this is similar to inner urge because it is the only quality I'm aware of communicating.

Finished. Pause. And then a miracle.

One I will forever carry in an unspeakably intimate place—a place into which no ray of light has entered for ten long years, not since I gaily sang "Matchmaker, matchmaker, make me a match" at my college audition for *Fiddler on the Roof* and, instead of winning the role of ingenue, got cast as the corpse Grandma Tzeitel.

As if in slow motion, Brida explodes from her desk, an intense, mesmerized expression on her face, and I see her hand plummet down in front of her with something in it. The object swims before me, inviting, enigmatic, then suddenly melts into focus. It is a badly Xeroxed map of Hollywood.

"Here is a map which shows you where the two-day intensive acting workshop is that I want you to attend, so you can be out auditioning for commercials as soon as possible!" Brida burns with conviction. "You are marvelous! Really, really marvelous. What energy! And I want you to have your photos done immediately. I'm giving an excellent photographer your phone number so he can hook up with you for a session right away."

She pauses and catches her breath: "I'm going to try and get you into 'The Book'!"

.   .   .

Our acting instructor, Lynn, sits unobtrusively in the back of the room. Fluorescent lights glare overhead. There is a video camera set up in one corner.

As an acting exercise, we are to talk *Chorus Line*-esque about ourselves for two minutes—who we are, where we're going.

We are:

Scott, twenty, a service adviser at Texaco. He has spent two years in the Navy and studied to be a paramedic. Faces International represents an important career step for him.

Claire, approximately nineteen, a nurse. She is here because she likes to travel, and she believes Faces International will help her get a career in which she does so.

Vincent has driven trucks for ten years. He figures he can always drive trucks. But if he doesn't give acting his best shot now, how will he ever know if he could have made it or not?

Robert, thirty-two, is a mortgage banker. He has one child.

Donna is twenty-two. She has been married twice, no kids. She loves pickup trucks and raises Pomeranians.

Henry is from Romania. He works as an airport controller. Since he was a child, he wanted to act in commercials. For him, Faces International represents a dream coming true.

Holly, sixteen, is a graduate of John Casablancas. After she graduates from high school, maybe she'll enroll at a two-year college, but she doesn't want to get involved in a four-year program in case the thing with Faces International takes off.

For the next two days, in addition to Lynn's detailed critiques of our eight-to-ten commercials, each before the video camera, we learn what to do when the director says, "Hit your mark," "Slate your name," "Action," and "Cut." We're shown a "T" drawn in masking tape on the floor and the importance of standing on it (so that one remains on camera at all times). Pre-audition breathing exercises are practiced. "Coloring" the text with voice inflection, pitch, and phrasing is explored.

Nor does the business aspect of launching a career in commercial acting go unnoticed. Helpful books are recommended. Managers and unions are mentioned. We're informed that, aside from having an agent, headshots are crucial, as is an acting résumé. Lynn gives instructions in how to write a résumé with no acting credits. (Under "Special Abilities," one of her former students lists "Lip-sync contest winner, local clubs." Another uses "Lifeguard, personable.")

$535 later ($300 for the acting workshop, $235 for my photos, care of "Fashion Photographs by Jihad"), I sit with my fellow Faces International soon-to-be graduates. While we all feel great about what Faces International has done for us (already Robert's talent counselor wants to send him out on auditions; Vincent's has promised him a personal introduction to two well-known agents), there is some slight disagreement over the cost of space in the August 1990 book.

Strangely enough, not one of us has yet seen a price sheet. Talent counselors have taken evasive action throughout. Consequently, word-of-mouth is now wildly conflicting. Henry says his half-page is costing him only $500, whereas Robert, with some concern, says he's supposed to come up with $1,500. Vincent was told he is getting a 2 x 2 (one-twelfth of a page) for $185, but intrepid Donna has measured the one-twelfth of a page and says they're a lot closer to 1½ x 1½. No matter. Donna's boyfriend (who makes $40,000 a year after taxes, she proudly informs us, by driving a Dy-Dee Diaper truck) will cover hers, regardless of what it ends up costing.

Henry will be graciously granted a three-day extension from Faces International the following Monday when he finds out his information was in error. He claims he will have no trouble securing a $1,500 bank loan to cover his presentation in the book, philosophizing, "You gotta spend money to make money." His main frustration is that his on-camera work was not better. He stumbled over words on the cue card and had trouble with simple directorial instructions, e.g., doing his gestural "button" (a thumbs-up, "We're No. 1" look) and taking a sip of soda at the same time. He also has kind of a heavy accent ("Boorger King," "chizboorger," "translator radio" instead of transistor radio). Lynn, whose credits include a guest-star on *Knots Landing* (girlfriend of the man who fell in love with Val when she had amnesia) and a featured role in *Cat People* (she falls down a flight of stairs screaming; they had to shoot it seventeen times—one acting anecdote she shares with us), advises patience. As she repeats doggedly, over and over again, "Acting is like playing basketball. You have to practice and practice and practice. Be easy on yourself. Remember that you've only been doing this one day!"

Five of my photos are out on Brida's desk. Is she excited. Great news! The board has met, and they've okayed me for up to a full color page. Unfortunately, the deadline for the August book is today.

Lo and behold, the magic binder opens, and the Faces International price list materializes.

	Color	B/W
$1/12$ page	n/a	$ 495
$1/4$ page	$1,350	$ 995
$1/2$ page	$3,150	$2,450
Full (4 pics)	$4,450	$3,300
Full (5 pics)	$4,650	$3,500

True, my five photographed "new looks" are impressive for a person whose driver's license photo was so unflattering the DMV actually took it upon itself to mail a second one. I especially take note of "Sandra Loh, TV anchorwoman." Instead of the microphone Lynn assigned me, I'm grinning into a telephone. Combine this with my hair and my dress, and rather than exuding Connie Chung, I look oddly like Mrs. Hernandez, who was my loan officer at Glendale Federal. However, the real Sandra Loh, the one with the checkbook, feels the sheer weight of the $4,650, as heavy as some kind of grotesque medicine ball Brida has thrown. "It's just that I . . . that I don't think I can get that kind of money together tonight," is how I begin, slowly, to try and ease myself out of what could be a bad situation.

Before my very eyes, my former-model pal and cheerleader Brida transmogrifies. From flawless British *Vogue* beauty to a disfiguring Lucifer in *Paradise Lost,* Brida becomes an incredible swirling evil. Could her commission from Faces International be that much?

"How about your credit card?" She is chattering, picking up

speed. "Why don't I just run it through? You can bring in a check tomorrow, eight A.M. sharp, and we'll tear up the slip—tear it right up—but then you'll have the space guaranteed."

Using my two days of acting training, I attempt lying hysterically. "If I don't get the money in tonight, why don't I try for the next time around?"

"August is the month when everything is happening! Everything! It's just that I think you could be out there right now." The sinews in Brida's neck are working overtime. "Auditioning! Making money!" She's hit the shriek level with the last phrase.

"Why don't you put $495 down—just $495 for a twelfth of a page. That way I can reserve a spot for you—it's just that our bookkeeper is so picky—and later we can trick the computer—you know, trick the computer into thinking it was a whole page."

My breath is coming in gasps.

"Sandra," Brida says, immediately changing tacks, trying to dredge up some charm in the midst of an ocean of bitterness, "I'd like to introduce you to Laurence DeBoulange, the National Director of Talent for Faces International." How can the formerly fabulous Brida be stooping to the most clichéd of used-car ruses, the "I have Mr. Bernstein, President of West Coast Sales on the line" trope?

The silver-haired Laurence Deboulange materializes with eerie, almost-as-if-he's-been-listening-outside-the-door speed. "I've just checked on the computer for you," he informs Brida, with hushed deference. "And as you suspected, space for the August book is very, very tight. What I've done is put in a little question mark," he says, nodding at me, "next to *Sahn*dra's name. Just a little—a little question mark. Of course, sometimes we do withdraw people from the book if we feel they're not worth it. But in your case," his smile is steely, "you deserve to be in." When I leave Brida and Laurence Deboulange without having committed, they look as if they're in rehearsal for the climax of *Scanners.*

Hollywood is cruel. One day you walk out of Faces International a star. The next week you're afraid to answer your phone. Faces International calls me seven times in twenty-four hours regarding the deadline for the August book.

In the city of a thousand scams—"swimsuit" photographers, "nonunion" agents, and "close friends" of producers, all of whom would like you to stop by after dinner—at least Faces International is up-front about the fact that it can't guarantee you either work or an agent. And somehow, some important need is being fulfilled. At $3 million a book, if you count photos and multiply by the appropriate rates, Faces International's book grosses $12 million a year, because willing prospects keep streaming in.

Dear Faces:

Faces has given me an experience I will never forget. If nobody picks me for anything, just being in the magazine is good enough.

Ron Wylie Jr.
Connersville, Indiana

Perhaps if I had spent the $4,650 (in addition to the $535, bringing the total invested to $5,185), Eddie Murphy Productions would have called me, offering me $2 million to shave my head.

Now I'll never get those bookend Oscars. I'll never get to tear down Jimmy Stewart's house and put up something bigger. Here I sit, poor, revved up, filled with inner urge. Wait a second, Where's the matchbook that said "Draw me" on the cover? I had it here a minute ago.

How to
Become Famous

The American mass media is organized in such a way that any reasonably clever citizen can become famous overnight, and on a shoestring budget, too. In addition, as we will see, Los Angeles is the best place in the country to nurture the kind of fame you make yourself. Armed only with a handful of press releases, you can create your own little globe of notoriety, which can radiate outward from a blurb in the "Only in L.A." column of the *Los Angeles Times* to an interview on NPR, a photo-essay in the *National Enquirer*, or even a full-blown live appearance on *The Tonight Show.*

Unless you are prepared to spend the rest of your life in jail or to die in an electric chair, though, you must face up to the fact that you will never become quite as famous through performing a single act as Sirhan Sirhan. And yet, performing a single awe-inspiring action in a public place—even if it isn't a felony—can still get you on the evening news and put your photo on the Associated Press wire, which can lead to feature articles, to Tawny Little mispronouncing your name, and to phone calls at odd hours of the day from sleazy, rabid radio talk-show hosts in far-flung outposts such as Kansas, Denver, or even Ouagadougou. It can even lead beyond—to *People* magazine itself.

How to Make the Evening News

So how does one go about it? How does one make the evening news without the benefit of having anything important to say, without inside connections, without a grant, a sugar daddy, a po-litical cause even? Having no objective in mind but the widespread propagation of your own image poses an arresting rhetorical chal-lenge when it comes to wording your press releases—which are essentially advertising copy geared to persuade local news crews to bypass the hard news at City Hall and expend costly man-power and film stock on you.

Lacking any social relevance, the only selling point you have is that you will give great video. It then becomes something of a sci-ence to think of visually spectacular single acts that will irre-sistably compel reporters and photographers to jump into their cars and come on down. On a purely aesthetic level, you should think of a scene bursting with color and motion—a conga line a thousand people long, a chemical explosion of some kind, some-thing or someone plummeting seven stories, preferably in flames.

Unless your action is in celebration of a national holiday or some other topical matter—the Fourth of July, the anniversary of the Hula-hoop, a record-breaking heat wave—you will probably also need to incorporate a hard-news element into your performance.

1. *Use a location fraught with symbolism.* Doing something appropriate at the Hollywood sign or before the Federal Building will lend what was previously an ordinary action great significance and meaning, and makes a readily identifiable setting. Also, a wide-angle shot of a resonant landmark is the perfect way to open a news clip—half the story is already there.

2. *Do something that provokes interaction with the public, possibly at great danger to yourself.* What was previously a stagey, symbolic action becomes actual news, merely because of the unpredictability and sometimes violent nature of crowds. Danger creates an atmosphere of Geraldo Rivera-like tension—i.e., great live television.

Since you are in competition with a whole nation's worth of moving pictures, make sure the scene is camera-ready. Do not be shy about checking out your site beforehand and thinking through, if not rehearsing, possible camera angles. Make sure direct sunlight falls on everything: consider selecting a location where a few palm trees will appear in the background—it's a nice touch that lets viewers on the East Coast know that this spectacle is live from Southern California, which many will find deeply terrifying.

Media outlets in other parts of this country—who will be seeing your photo if it goes out on the Associated Press wire—consider Los Angeles to be largely populated by self-promoting yahoos. This is a terrific advantage, as you are operating in an already well-established genre—no one need interview you directly to understand your motivation. Through one picture, the story has arrived ready and complete from Los Angeles, a story about a wild and crazy person doing a publicity stunt in order to get attention and a possible job from people in the entertainment industry!

In the same vein, Hollywood is really the best Los Angeles location to perform your action. In a nation of mass-media outlets where complex messages must be conveyed in as few words as possible, a story that contains the highly resonant code-word "Hollywood" will travel farther than, let's say, one that contains the infrequently used code-word "Alhambra." If you can throw in some wacky new twist on the New Age, so much the better—it is what people on the East Coast expect from Southern Californians, and will therefore be a story they pass around to each other with great energy.

In a sense, we in Los Angeles are the most honest and the most highly evolved citizens of a nation of self-promoters. Folks in Denver or Kentucky have to pull a child out of a well or grow an enormous glandular pumpkin to get their moments of glory. Thanks to the likes of Angelyne, we can head directly, unapologetically, for the grail itself.

How to Make
the National
"Wacky News" Circuit

There exists an entire subgenre of news, on both the local and national levels, that can be characterized as Wacky News. The man who can paint sunsets in five minutes, a doctor who claims he knows what dinosaurs sounded like, pig-racing in Iowa, the Bra Museum—these are all good examples of Wacky News, humorous blurbs that can fill up the odd-sized bit of space with offbeat, incongruous headlines, and are chock-full of one-liners.

The ideal Wacky Person is naively unselfconscious, very enthusiastic, and deeply sincere; he or she provides a lot of unintentionally hilarious details and seems unaware that the reporter is making the best jokes. A lot of these people seem to flourish in places like the Midwest. A lot of them make it onto *The Tonight Show.*

This is your news circuit, so you might as well get to know it.

L.A. Times

In the *L.A. Times,* the most consistent outlet for Wacky News is "Only in L.A./People and Events" (Metro section, page two). It's a good place to send a press release because in a sense it's not that competitive; out of five tidbits, usually three are reasonably diverting, and the other two just kind of fall flat. Sometimes the ironies or moments the writers seem to be reaching for take more time to explain than they are really worth. Apparently, there is a shortage of good material out there!

Are the people of Los Angeles simply not lively enough to keep that column hilarious on a daily basis? At this juncture, it seems that we as a city can do only enough outrageous things to keep a column of about half that length filled. The other half is largely made up of Unusual Coincidences or Funny Olympics of some sort or another, which generally lack a satisfying punch.

However, writers and photojournalists from other publications do keep an eye on that column, which is why it's worth getting into. A freelance journalist looking for the quick Wacky Story will skim it to make sure he/she hasn't missed anything; at least one photojournalist from the *National Enquirer* reads that column.

Steve Harvey is a particularly good person to send press releases to in the Metro section. He seems to have an unending appetite for things Wacky, and will occasionally do an entire piece on some such person.

Herald Examiner

The thing to note about the *Herald* is that it greatly lags behind the *Times* in circulation, which means that they have to sell a lot of papers and sell them fast. Whereas the front-page photo of the *Times* is usually relegated to the latest plane crash in Armenia or to some major foreign dignitary making a historic speech of some kind, the *Herald* will throw colorful local stuff on the front page with shrieking headlines—anything to get somebody to put a quarter in the box.

Stories that get three column inches on page 5 of the *Times* Metro section can show up on the front page of the *Herald* if they think it'll capture your imagination. The little girl who got dragged quite a distance along the ground because of a wayward kite made the front page of the *Herald*, for instance. *I* made the front page of the *Herald* a week before I did a piano concert at the Harbor Freeway, complete with a particularly lurid close-up of my face and the liberally paraphrased quote: "I think my brain is a little mixed-up."

Send a press release to the *Herald*, therefore, at your own peril. You just may make the front page. Interestingly, a lot of foreign journalists seem to read the *Herald*.

People

Todd Gold of the Los Angeles bureau of *People* always sounds curt and suspicious when he picks up his phone, and it's no wonder. He gets deluged with mail and phone calls every week from people who want to be in *People*, people who sometimes include airplane tickets and other such bribes, etc. It's probably best to send a press release and leave the man alone.

People will profile a Wacky Person, but you have to have been doing it for a while. In addition, you have to be at peace with your Wackiness—they want gutsy iconoclasts with a down-home sense of humor, not pathetic, confused misfits of society. Not to say that they won't cover people in the latter category, but that's a different kind of story—you usually have to have a heart-breaking rare and fatal disease to make it in that way, and be waging some kind of bitter lawsuit.

Even though you are a Wacky Person rather than a bona fide celebrity, they may still want to interview you in your living room, particularly if it is a Wacky one. If you let them, of course, make sure your living room is camera-ready.

Wall Street Journal

Dan Akst, Los Angeles entertainment writer for the *Wall Street Journal*, is one of those amazing journalists who is desperately busy but who also opens and reads all his mail. It's worth it to mail to the *Wall Street Journal* because of the "orphan" (second section, front page, lower left-hand corner), a column exclusively devoted to things Wacky. This is a terrific place to be in because *everybody* reads the *Journal*. You get into that column and you're fully in the national Wacky News circuit—NPR is right around the corner!

Since the terribly well-educated and verbally brilliant writers at the *Journal* use other people's Wackiness to brilliantly and subtly expose deep ironies of twentieth-century American culture, you'll be in capable hands. They can make a stone come off as hilariously postmodern by virtue of its implacable silence. All of your quotes will be slickly truncated so you sound understated, wry, and dreadfully, dreadfully witty.

The Tonight Show

To get on the show, it seems that you need a gimmick that can be carried in your purse or brought onto a small stage—a bag of unusual nuts, something like that, or performing animals. Also, it's best if you appear sincere and completely unconscious of your own irony—this leaves Johnny lots of room to deadpan, make hilarious understatements, etc.

As a point of illustration, when I did my freeway piano concert I was on the same news circuit as a team of racing pigs from Iowa. They were in the *Wall Street Journal* "orphan" the day after me;

and they were on the same NPR show as I was (along with a man who could paint sunsets in five minutes). In that magical week and a half of fame, in every national media outlet in which I saw my own name there was an even better and sometimes longer story about those pigs.

The key point here is while for a brief time my notoriety was locked in a death grip with that of the pigs, the pigs eventually surpassed me in fame. While I was worth only a few jokes in Johnny Carson's monologue, the pigs were the ones who actually made it onto the show. A lesson of some kind may be gleaned from this.

National Enquirer

The *National Enquirer* is the most aesthetically pure of national publications. They care less about why you're doing something than if it will make a stunning picture—expect to be quizzed rigorously on every visual detail before a photographer is actually assigned to your story, down to what color you will be wearing and the direction of the sun.

One thing to know about the *Enquirer* is they like to have photo exclusives. If a good picture of your event goes out on the Associated Press wire, they're less likely to run the story.

Five Rules for
Appearing on
the Evening News

Getting on:

1. *Date of your event:* Try not to do anything on a day when the pope or some other major dignitary is visiting, or on a news-saturated day such as Super Tuesday.

Unfortunately, you can't always predict when a slow news day will be. Unforeseen events may come up and elbow you out of precious news time. Hijackings and other terrorist actions are especially bad—not only do they demand a lot of television time, but they put everyone in a grim and ponderous mood. Also annoying are fires breaking out in the city, or other natural disasters, which make terrific video.

Friday is a good day of the week—you have an opportunity to get on the weekend news as well.

2. *Time of your event:* Schedule your event at noon or earlier. This gives crews plenty of time to edit the tape and even make a teaser for four o'clock. Also, bear in mind that, if CNN does come down, the East Coast is three hours later than we are.

3. *Location of your event:* Many of the local news stations are on Sunset Boulevard in Hollywood. Picking a location as close as possible to that is greatly to your advantage.

4. *What to wear:* Given a choice, a bright color will add visual interest to color slide photos and television.

5. *What to say:* Inevitably, you will be asked *why*. By all means, keep it short. If you do not, what you say will be edited right out or edited peculiarly—in any case, it will seem dull, you

will seem very confused, and none of it will make any sense whatsoever when you finally see it on television.

BAD: Why am I doing this? I'm a conceptual artist deeply interested in exploring the notion of the truly postmodern work in which the medium is the message and *langue* is not *parole,* my metaphor for the ultimate degeneracy of meaning being television. Creating a performance specifically for the evening news is, I believe, an utterly self-reflexive act; since this is a media-created event, and the media is covering this event, well, I see it as a forum which implodes problematically onto itself. . . .

GOOD: Why am I doing this? I don't know! Just to have some fun, I guess! (Smile broadly and wave. Cut.)

Hey, Gang,
It's *Baywatch*

Every time I click back to *Baywatch*—the most popular TV show on the planet—it's like I never left it at all.

Kites are still flying; joggers are still jogging; the Pacific is still blue. A banner stretched across the lifeguard station reads: BIG KAYAK RACE TOMORROW! Below stand a pair of clean-shaven youths in red swim trunks. Under the glare of the white sun, they wear the classic *Baywatch* beach-squint.

What can these two young Adonises be saying? We move in closer. We listen.

"But will C.J. and Summer make it back in time for the race?" asks one, pushing a strand of blond hair off his forehead.

"I don't know!" The hands of the other go up.

Two young women in thong bikinis and kneepads Rollerblade by, with a kind of regal stiffness. One squats briefly, rises again.

"How about Mitch? Can he do it?"

"No!" Emphatic head shake. "He's doing CPR training in San Diego . . . with Hobie!"

"Really?"

"Yes!"

"But we've been waiting *all year* to—"

Oh, it doesn't really matter what the words are. Not for Noël Coward quips do Brazilians in mud huts hook their generators up, ritualistically, at three in the afternoon. Emmy-winning writing or no, it's not *Murphy Brown* that reigns as the No. 1 U.S.-imported show in England, Germany, France, Australia. Wisecracking Dennis Miller can take all the shots he wants. ("I have a little crick in my neck from watching David Hasselhoff hold his stomach in on *Baywatch*!") It still won't make his one of the top syndicated shows in the U.S., after things *Star Trek*.

No, *Baywatch* is what the world is tuned to. Now in its fifth season, it is estimated that almost a billion people gather round to watch it every week. Eighty episodes later, with syndication covering 98 percent of U.S. markets, the formula still hasn't gone flat.

Flat is hardly the word, you say? It's more like a weekly buns-o-rama? May we beg to differ. A common misperception about *Baywatch* is that it is strictly a T&A show. The word is *strictly*. Yes, it's filmed on Southern California beaches. Yes, it is chock-full of slo-mo sequences of hunks running along the water. Yes, the percentage of silicone breasts is probably at least 75 percent. So what? This is L.A. Believe me, you would regret it if there weren't silicone in them there hooters.

As you would if there were no Red Suit, the "uniform" of the show's female lifeguards. Before, we used to think of the bikini as the most gravitationally challenging of swimsuits. Now we know that's 50 percent wrong. (*Baywatch* is syndicated in so many markets and number one in so many strange foreign lands that one feels an out-of-control need to use more and more statistics.)

The fact is that bikini tops have definite underwire possibilities. Not so the *Baywatch* Red Suit—that devilish little one-piece that former *Playboy* cover girl Pamela Anderson ("C. J. Parker") has made famous in more than one hundred countries. Breasts must look alert and alive on their own merits, trapeze artists without a net. Legs? The legs of the Red Suit are cut so high and deep, even the leanest female bum looks like a zaftig peach.

Without the mighty trio of silicone, liposuction, and electrolysis, few average women would dare take up the gauntlet hurled down by the Red Suit. No, most of us would lope along the beach, chin grimly down on our chests, holding one breast in each hand. (Let's not even *think* the phrase *yeast infection*.) No wonder most of us aren't on *Baywatch*. And . . . aren't you glad?

But there is much more to *Baywatch* than the Bayberati that garnish it. This is an hour-long show, after all; after a moment's titillation (all *Baywatch* will give you, just that moment), soft-porn junkies will get bored. They'll find themselves sitting through long talks between lifeguard Mitch (David Hasselhoff) and teen son Hobie (Jeremy Jackson). Lieutenant Stephanie Holden (Alexandra Paul) will comfort buffed-out lifeguard Matt (David Charvet) by crying out, with oddly fierce cheer: "Let's go work out! Come on!" Even Pamela Anderson will pull on a sweater and go off to save whales.

What's really at the heart of *Baywatch* turns out to be good old-fashioned storytelling—*old* old-fashioned. We're talking Ancient Greece when actors donned huge masks and clogs and yelled at thousands of drunken revelers on a hill with not-so-keen attention spans. *Baywatch* plot turns have that same yelled quality, because now the village is global. Stories need to hold their shape all the way out to Outer Mongolia.

For dramatic development, there is ye good olde Clunk o' the Mast to the Forehead. How many of the unsuspecting go sailing in *Baywatch* only to turn suddenly over an ominous swell in the music and crack their noggin on an errant yardarm? With a wail, they lose consciousness and crumple backward into the sea.

A great example of Clunk o' the Mast to the Forehead occurs when Mitch is visited by errant brother Buzzy. Buzzy wants to ditch his teen son so he can sail around the world. Mitch is outraged. Buzzy is outraged at his outrage. Just when it seems the scene has nowhere else to go, the mast swings round and—*Clunk!*—Buzzy hurtles into the sea. "Buzzy!" Mitch howls.

A troubled family needs healing. Only The Sea can help.

Clunk o' the Mast to the Forehead works so well, you miss it when they try to vary the formula. One episode featured Hobie jumping off his Jet Ski, only to be attacked by a . . . jellyfish. Most jellyfish are pie-size, 98 percent water, and are relatively harmless. Yet the music swelled determinedly as a cold sore. The Hobster flailed and lost consciousness. "Clunk o' the Mast to the Forehead!" you wanted to cry out. We love it! We expect it! Don't mess with success!

After crisis comes dramatic resolution—via the de rigueur CPR scene. The message is clear: Denial of one's basic human need to Love and Care (or, "I'd rather spit than spend weekends with my son!") always produces maritime disaster; CPR enhanced by shock paddles to the chest provides psychic rebirth. The result is always success, followed by a tearful family reunion: "I didn't realize until now how much I love you!" Hug. Thumbs up. Twinkle. Roll credits.

"The key word with me is that I have good taste."

So says the guy with his thumb up, twinkle in his eye. Add curly brown hair, dimples, bronzed chest, collar on the red life-guard jacket turned up, and you will recognize David Hasselhoff. More than the show's star and co-executive producer, he is its moral center, its conscience, its voice. Hasselhoff is *Baywatch*. Hasselhoff's work on the small screen includes a six-year stint in the seventies as Snapper Foster on *The Young and the Restless* and, of course, as Michael Knight, the star of *Knight Rider*. From the latter, he draws two key stories that reveal what David Hassel-hoff brings to television.

"I was the one who turned *Knight Rider* into more of a comedy thing—into something charming and funny. It happened when I first called the car 'buddy' or 'pal,' and patted it like a horse." He raps the table. "'Let's go, pal!' It felt right. I was trying to emulate Burt Reynolds in *Smokey and the Bandit.*"

The other Great Moment involved a talk with Grant Tinker.

"We were walking in the parking lot one day, when *Knight Rider* was on. And he says, 'By the way, I'm Grant Tinker—head of CBS.' And I said, 'You know what? Will you please get our show close-captioned? I have a lot of deaf people coming up to me saying they can't understand the car.'

"He walked away, then walked back and said, 'Funny you

asked me that. You didn't ask for more money, or a motor home, or to complain. You asked me about the deaf kids.' "

Hasselhoff's passion for bringing otherly abled children and TV together is brought to bear today on *Baywatch*. His inspiration continues to be Michael Landon and "stories that make you cry." Hasselhoff's favorite ever *Baywatch* episode?

He thinks a moment, leans forward. His voice grows husky.

" 'The Child Inside,' with Special Olympics kids, starring Mary Lou Retton. Without a doubt, that week was the greatest one on *Baywatch*. The kids were hysterical! They were terrific—gave so much love. The heavyset black guy who carried the torch, he was always pointing at his heart and saying, 'I love *you*.'

"I was in Atlantic City doing my Pay-Per-View recently, and this handicapped girl walked up to me. She had a Special Olympics shirt on. And she says, 'I watched *Baywatch*. I went out and competed, and I won this for you.' And she put this medal around my neck! It was amazing, the magazine people—*GQ* and all that—couldn't believe the moment."

Don't *you* feel crappy? You, who dubbed this *The T&A Team*?

Hasselhoff is only one-quarter of the *Baywatch* producing team. The other 75 percent includes co-executive producers Doug Schwartz and Michael Berk. A team since childhood, their voices overlap as they describe why *they* think the show works.

"The two-hour pilot of *Baywatch* was called *Panic at Malibu Pier,* and was very successful. The problem was, the studio and the network could not agree on what the series should be. Was it *Murder on the Beach*? *CHiPs on the Beach*? "

"Also, one-hour shows are expensive. If you shoot them in nine days, costs can run up to $1.3 million per episode."

"So we took it over ourselves. We cut the budget to $830,000 by shooting each episode in five days instead of nine. We do this by doing first-unit and second-unit shots at the same time—so you don't have eighty guys sitting around on their duffs."

Another money saver is using shorter scripts—forty to fifty pages instead of sixty to seventy. To pad out the hour, co-executive producer Greg Bonann, a lifeguard with experience shooting Olympics footage, directs a lot of *Baywatch*'s "music video" montages—Jet Ski sequences, motorcycle sequences, wind-sailing and surfing, and body-boarding and beach walking, and . . .

Berk and Schwartz are cheerfully candid about who taught them the craft of producing. Their role model—on such pre-*Baywatch*, un–Michael Landonish projects as *Peace Killers, Psycho Psychos,* and *Sinner's Blood*—was Roger Corman, the legendary B-movie king.

The combination of four such wildly diverse aesthetics can be, Hasselhoff admits, "sometimes volatile." "There was a shot of Pamela Anderson crawling along the beach like a cat with the camera going up and down her . . . you know." It pains him to say it. "And I had to say, 'Guys, I'm going to have to explain this shot on every talk show. They're going to ask me, 'If this is not a T&A show, what is this?' I mean, I'm going to have to explain this to my mother!"

In truth, the magic formula here is Russ Meyer plus Michael Landon, *Little House on the Prairie* dropped onto *Beneath the*

Valley of the Ultra Vixens. To pass the Hasselhoff taste test, Pamela Anderson (Brigitte Bardot hair, pouty lips, sex-doll bod) must be "decency enhanced." Consider a typical shot of Anderson zagonga-ing down the beach. This is about sex, right?

Wrong.

"Never!" exclaims John D'Andrea, laughing. He and partner Cory Lerios compose the music for *Baywatch.* "It would be over the top! It would be redundant! It would be ridiculous!"

Unlike slutty ol' *Models Inc.*, which has groping, leering saxophones blowing all over, this is strictly a daytime, feel-good, *guitar* show.

Plus . . . where is Anderson running? Toward a Lost Child. When she gets to him, the master tableau is complete. Anderson squats—as she does so magnificently, bleached blond hair flowing over eruptive cleavage—next to the child. She circles her arm around the tot and murmurs comfort. For the coup de grâce, we garnish the child with, *all right,* a leg brace.

There. That's what Hasselhoff calls "*broad*-casting—appealing to a wide range of audiences."

That's what you call . . . *Baywatch* taste.

Of course, all this is familiar to viewers by now. What of the future?

Where do you go after four seasons of TV perfection?

To the fifth season, of course. Forty-four more episodes of *Baywatch* have been ordered. Jet Skis must be jumped onto, boats fallen off of, shock paddles rubbed frantically together. History will continue to be made—not at Hollywood and Vine, but at Pacific Coast Highway and Chautauqua.

Here, on the *Baywatch* set, kites are flying, joggers are jogging, and the ocean is blue.

The curve of white sand stretches on to infinity.

Trailers flank the parking lot like covered wagons huddled against Indian attack.

Up above, the sun blazes.

Faced with this morning's public-relations duties, most of the cast come through like pros. In trailer one, Pamela Anderson easily shares her enthusiasm about the acting classes she began eight months ago, her dog Star, Carl Jung, and her hobbies: writing poetry and painting. In trailer two, Alexandra Paul speaks articulately about her avid environmentalism and the wonderful camaraderie among the *Baywatch* cast. Neatly supporting both themes, enter jaunty new cast member Jaason Simmons. Simmons is an Australian from Tasmania—which somehow equals blond Caucasian. He has a teasing recycling question for Paul: "At home, I've got a stack of *Baywatch* scripts two feet high! Do I take them to the Dumpster or no?"

Sunbathing on the sand is Yasmine Bleeth, the other new cast member. "I'm working on my tan," she jokes, lifting a pale wrist. "It's part of my job!" She says she's tickled to be off her soap in New York. She points at the Pacific: "When I have an hour off, I'm not stuck in my dressing room on West 66th Street."

But not all performers draw energy from the white beach. Not all float easily before the phalanx of butt-crack guys that form the mighty crew of *Baywatch*: the cameramen, electricians, and grips eating roast-beef sandwiches and reading *Trucking* magazine.

Consider, for example, the *Baywatch* "Breck girls," a cadre of junior-varsity Pamela Andersons with long, fluffy hair and regulation cheek-baring Red Suits. They are typically called upon to "flesh out" CPR scenes—crowding round, handing up towels, raising eyebrows in concern. Though they sometimes have names, they almost never have lines.

Still, it takes something extra to get to wear the Red Suit. There are dozens of equally nubile females—Rollerblading, jogging, volleyballing across the set—who enjoy no such honor. Brunette April Gauthier reveals she landed her spot by winning the Miss *Baywatch* contest. ("We jogged, we swam, stuff like that.") Model and hairdresser Julie Cole is something of a celebrity herself. *Star* paparazzi recently snapped her in tight red minidress on the arm of Edd "Kookie" Byrnes from 77 *Sunset Strip,* whose current age is sixty.

Today, the aspiring actresses have waited in the punishing heat for hours. They're not sure they'll get to do a scene at all. In their crotch-pinching Red Suits, they sigh, shade their eyes, squint into the eternal sun.

Wilting in the heat, too, is the "background talent." These are the extras whose job it is to Cavort Ceaselessly on the sand, sunning, running, throwing Frisbees back and forth in Sisyphean rhythm. Today's beachgoers *look* right—in their baggy beach shorts, tennis visors, Hawaiian shirts, and bikinis.

But as soon as the scene requires them to act—rather, react—the facade drops, revealing them as the faux funsters they really are. A running lifeguard is cued. Tape rolls. He whips by the crowd in panic. But when he does so, they freeze. It's not a freeze of horror, they just . . . stop. After a moment's thought, they turn slowly, confused, cockroaches spritzed by Raid.

"Honestly," says director of photography James Pergola distastefully. "It's like *Night of the Living Dead* out there."

A certain exhaustion has gripped the remainder of the cast as well. Stud-muffin David Charvet cannot be coaxed from his trailer for a chat. The former Bugle Boy model, whose press kit says he tours local schools giving antidrug speeches, is not media-ready this afternoon. "He's sleeping. He's really tired."

Likewise, Jeremy Jackson—who plays Hobie and in person is growing noticeably taller and less cherubic than Hobie past—does not play child star today. Fourteen now, his interests lean more toward hanging out with his friends and less toward dishing platitudes about *Baywatch*. "Write down what you want," he offers.

"When Jeremy first auditioned, he was freaky positive to get this role!" is Hasselhoff's perspective. "But the older he's getting, the more scattered he is, and the more he's not really concentrating. I'm trying to get him back to his former energy." Nicole Eggert, who played buxom blonde Summer Quinn until last season, has bailed from the scene entirely.

"I think Nicole left the show for two reasons," Hasselhoff says. "She said she wanted to do . . . more important story lines, or more significant work, or something like that."

The king of syndicated television lets the words hang in the air. After a second, they take on a kind of irony.

He breezes on: "The main thing is, the first time we put her in the water, she said, '*God,* it's cold!' It wasn't even cold! We put her on a boat and she turned green. We've learned from those experiences. The first thing we ask now is, 'Can you swim?' Because we've had people take roles who could not swim. Good-looking actresses, great actresses, but you put them in the water and, whoa!

"Also, Nicole trashed the show on television and in reviews and stuff. And that wasn't cool. We have a saying on this show, 'If you pout, you're out.'"

Hasselhoff understands wanderlust, as he, too, has career interests outside *Baywatch*. He regularly tours Europe as a pop singer, is working on a new album, and recently starred in his own Pay-Per-View concert, shot in Atlantic City. (Unfortunately, it aired the same day a certain white Ford Bronco led police on a tour of Southern California freeways. "We got killed by the O. J. thing," he freely admits.)

Recent dramatic roles, too, are of a tenor quite different than that of the fatherly Mitch he plays on *Baywatch*. He just finished shooting a movie called *Avalanche*, in which he plays a "happy psycho." And he's really excited about the prospect of donning corset and heels to play Dr. Frank N. Furter in *The Rocky Horror Picture Show,* in either an L.A. or New York stint.

But all that's just moonlighting. He knows which side his bread is buttered on. TV-wise, he is sticking to the tried and true. Next up then is *Baywatch*'s first spin-off: *Baywatch Nights*. It will star Hasselhoff and *Baywatch*'s only black cast member, Gregory Alan-Williams.

"We open up a private investigation agency—we have a *Lethal Weapon* relationship. Instead of driving a hot car, we're going to have an old '68 Cadillac. We will deal with all the incredible stuff that takes place down here at night. It's dangerous as hell. The stuff on the pier, gangs, turf wars, tourists coming in, the drug scene—it all comes out at night.

"But for me," says the first man in TV history to call his car Buddy, "it will really have an emphasis on comedy."

So far, the rest of the *Baywatch* cast has been somewhat more reluctant to commit. "They're still trying to work out the numbers with all the players. But I'm sure that in the end everybody will wake up and smell the coffee. In the off-season, it's fine that they all go off and do their other projects and I go off and do mine. Sure. If you keep this base, you can always do other things."

He stabs another piece of melon with his fork. The waves continue to crash outside his trailer. Twenty feet away, a "Rubber Ducky," this season's new oceangoing rescue toy, is being readied for the next scene.

"Everyone has to realize that nothing—not my music nor their other projects—comes close to the success of this. Because the hit here really is *Baywatch*." He repeats simply, "*Baywatch* is the hit."

L.A.
Party Girls:
Wilder
Than Ever!

Los Angeles is a fetid maw full of stench.

Bony-faced, angry twelve-step actresses who fly into a rage if someone else sips a beer. TV composers in "keyboard" scarves who ply dinner guests with demo tapes of their *Rescue 911* sound cues. Goateed Eurotrash stylists who smoke in your bathroom, hiss through yellow teeth: "Leenda Evangelista—she iss beauti-fool. But Ceendy, she iss a beetch! I weel not werk wiss her. No."

When the flop sweat of this desperate town becomes just too nauseating, you drive up to Big Sur in a taut silence. You rent a cabin among rustling pines. You pull on a huge fluffy sweater and crunch down a red dirt trail toward the sea. You stare into the pearl-gray, wintery skies with narrowed eyes.

Tossing aside a peeled stick, you suddenly cry out:

"Why do we live in L.A.? I'm sick of it. Look how beautiful it is up here! The air smells so-o-o great, so fresh. Let's move to Big Sur! I'll bet I can get some kind of sixty-thousand-a-year consult-for-Fortune-500-companies-over-the-Internet-on-a-part-time-basis-from-your-home type job. Deal. Thingee."

Then you check your messages. And learn that one of your tiny, greasy little ships has come in.

And you throw back your head and cackle like Lucifer. Because there it is again. Work! The rush of . . . getting it. So what if it's Rotten Work for Bad Money, which will only lead to even more Rotten Work for Even Less Money. Think of all the people you *beat* to *get* this Stinky Bad Work! Ha ha ha!

"It's an article for *Cosmopolitan* called 'L.A. Party Girls: Wilder Than Ever!'" I crowed to a friend. Just one day earlier I'd sworn I was moving to Telluride, Colorado. But it's pricey there. You need a pile of Fetid L.A. Money to buy all the stuff: A-frame lodge, Adirondack furniture, Timberland boots. Wiser for now to stay the tawdry course, grow my Adirondack bundle.

"'L.A. Party Girls: Wilder Than Ever!'?" John was amazed. John is a serious East Coast journalist: the *Atlantic Monthly* is always interested in what he thinks about politics and the global economy. Fine. If L.A. Party Girls are ever the topic, I'm sure it is I who will be called. "How wild were they before? How wild are they now? How do you even measure something like that?"

See how lost John is in the world of women's magazines? He doesn't get the timeless quality of Topics We Love to Read About, like "Nails, Nails, Nails!" "What Doctors Aren't Telling Us About Yeast Infections!" and "Big Breasts Are Back IN!" He doesn't believe astrology is an actual subject. He can't relate to

Woman's Day-esque holiday cover "personalities" made entirely of cream cheese frosting.

"What happened to moving to Telluride?" he asked. "Why are you still doing this, this . . . L.A. party trash?"

I'm growing my Adirondack bundle! I wanted to fling back. Excuse me if *I'm* a professional with a job to do, for cash. Excuse me if that job is finding out everything about the L.A. Party Girl and sharing it with the American public. Twenty more jobs like this, and I'll be sitting pretty in Colorado.

So, whistling, I set to work. And here is what I found:

The L.A. Party Girl lives in Beverly Hills or West Hollywood. She is twenty-five or younger. She has the best hair! She hangs out with Nicolette Sheridan by the pool. Nicolette is really, really nice. Shopping at Jess Maddox is a must. Iranians are weird. There's this guy named Pez who's kind of a pest. The trick is to let him buy you a drink and ditch him.

I thought there was a lot of great stuff here. Also in my notebook I had: "Shoes by Maud Frizon," "Trader Vic's on Friday nights can be really happening," "Scott Baio is totally horny."

But no. "What about Jack, Sly, Christian, Ethan?" my *Cosmo* editor exclaimed. "Scott Baio—who cares? Who *are* these girls?"

Oops. Obviously I needed better quality. True, one blue umbrella drink at Trader Vic's and these girls' foreheads hit the table. They were L.A. Party Girls, but were they Wilder Than Ever? They seemed a little tired; one said she was bloated from eating clams at Dantana's. In the meantime, sure, I'd gotten a line on some girls who'd hung with Sly, but . . .

"Okay," the editor agreed. "Drinks and appetizers at Eclipse. But that's it. *No* entrees. The bill will be killer."

So I and the newer, better L.A. Party Girls convene at our appointed Beverly Hills hot spot, ready to cut our deal.

Teri Smith has been designated lead Party Girl on the job. She will tell her story about putting her hand down Pauly Shore's pants in exchange for a big *Cosmo* photo of herself laughing. No photo for Jan and Kendra, Teri has agreed, just booze and snacks. Teri's friend Jonathan—former Elite model, now unemployed—will share some Sly anecdotes in exchange for being identified as "Jonathan Katz, Hollywood's hottest new interior designer."

I will profess interest in their miserable ratlike lives. I will obtain my fresh steaming celeb poop, convertible to cash.

We all seem cool. But the first tray of drinks comes and Jonathan waffles. He seems to crumple under his black Armani coat. He takes a tragic quaff of marguerita with wobbling hand.

"What if Sly gets mad?" he worries, now that tape's rolling. "I didn't tell Sly I was doing this. I've known him just two weeks. I don't want to blow a possible screenplay thing."

"Jonathan," Teri abjures flatly. "Just say, 'Sly is a great guy.' So you can be quoted. Get the publicity."

"But he's not!" Jonathan's flawless face becomes crafty. He leans in toward me, voice husky: "I can tell you stuff—"

"You *can't* launch a design company that way!" Teri hisses. "You have to say something nice! You're so *stupid*!"

"Maybe I just won't say anything!" he yells.

Big platters appear with lobster claws hanging off them.

Eight hands gleefully reach up.

"Surf 'n' turf?" I cry out, betrayed. "You *didn't*!"

Colorado, then, bobs ever farther from me. If I don't make it in the end, lay my body at Sunset and La Cienega. Put some Timberland boots on me, point my head toward Laurel Canyon. Never mind that the stars will be smoggy, Mercedes horns will be honking. Somewhere a breeze will be blowing, tinged with Bijan.

Sandra Tsing Loh has written "The Valley" column for *Buzz* magazine, and is a commentator on National Public Radio. As a solo performer, she has been featured in the HBO New Writers Project and at the U.S. Comedy Festival in Aspen. She has won a Pushcart Prize for Fiction and a MacDowell fellowship. Her writing has also appeared in *Glamour, Elle, Harper's Bazaar, Cosmopolitan,* and *The New York Times*. She is the author of a novel, *If You Lived Here, You'd Be Home By Now* and a comic monologue, *Aliens in America*.